Mindfulness and the 12 Steps

Thérèse Jacobs-Stewart

HAZELDEN®

Hazelden
Center City, Minnesota 55012
hazelden.org

Library of Congress Cataloging-in-Publication Data

Jacobs-Stewart, Thérèse.
  Mindfulness and the 12 steps / Thérèse Jacobs-Stewart.
     p. cm.
  Includes bibliographical references.
  ISBN 978-1-59285-820-0 (softcover)
  1. Twelve-step programs—Religious aspects—Buddhism. 2. Religious life—Buddhism. 3. Self-help techniques. I. Title. II. Title: Mindfulness and the twelve steps.
  BQ4570.T85J33 2010
  294.3'376229—dc22

                                                                    2010005720

Editor's note
The names, details, and circumstances may have been changed to protect the privacy of those mentioned in this publication.

This publication is not intended as a substitute for the advice of health care professionals.

Alcoholics Anonymous, AA, and the Big Book are registered trademarks of Alcoholics Anonymous World Services, Inc.

14 13 12 11   2 3 4 5 6

Cover design by Percolator
Interior design and typesetting by Madeline Berglund

Also by Thérèse Jacobs-Stewart

Paths Are Made by Walking:
Practical Steps for Attaining Serenity

I dedicate this book to the people who attend the Twelve Steps and Mindfulness meetings at Mind Roads Meditation Center in Saint Paul, Minnesota. We were inspired by the Meditation in Recovery group at San Francisco Zen Center, which in turn rests upon the awakening of countless beings going all the way back to the Buddha. In each moment of the unfolding conversation about recovery and mindfulness, we are supported by them. May wisdom, compassion, and serenity arise in all.

As a blind man feels
when he finds a pearl in the dust-bin,
so am I amazed by the miracle of awakening
rising in my consciousness.

From the "Bodhicharyavatara" by Shantideva[1]

CONTENTS

PREFACE

We meet Monday evenings at Mind Roads Meditation Center in Saint Paul, Minnesota, one chapter in a nationwide community of Twelve Steps and Mindfulness meetings. The room is soft with candlelight, scented by burning incense, and lined with black cushions on the polished oak floor. Our addictions are widespread: drugs, alcohol, food, gambling, cigarettes, or codependency. Everyone is welcome.

We introduce ourselves by going around the circle, saying our first name and Twelve Step affiliation. We have a common interest in meditation practices and how they can inform our recovery from addiction. Each month, we discuss one of the Twelve Steps and how Buddhist thought, meditation, and mindfulness practice can be applied to our life in recovery. We sit in silent meditation together, hear a talk by one of our members, and share our reflections.

As with many Twelve Step meetings, we are a diverse group of people, tall and short, wide and thin, black and white and brown. BMW sedans are parked next to rusty pickup trucks in the parking lot.

Yet we are part of the great stream of beings seeking deeper serenity in our lives, grounded in sobriety by the Twelve Step program, inspired to awaken and live in the present by the practices of mindfulness meditation. In our addictions, we were never here in the moment. We *wanted* to be gone. Now we are learning to wake up to the joy of being alive.

Once a month for the past five years, I have given a talk to our Monday night group. The following chapters are your virtual seat in our meeting. Please make yourself at home.

ACKNOWLEDGMENTS

The mind, hearts, and energy of many people contributed to the seeding of this book in me and its manifestation in the written form you now hold in your hands.

Bowing in thanksgiving to:

My loved ones, including: Jim, my dearest friend and partner of thirty years, and Cathie and Ted Furman, for their undying enthusiasm and care.

My fellow writers: Lindsay Nielsen, Sue McCauley, Astrid Slungaard, Darla Garvey, and Donna Karis, for their inspiration and invaluable feedback; my editors, Doug Toft and Sid Farrar, for their tremendous skill and the pure pleasure of working with them.

My spiritual advisers: Father Michael Winterer, Sister Mary Sharon Riley, Thrangu Rinpoche, Tenshin-roshi Reb Anderson, and Eijun Linda Ruth Cutts, for their deep wisdom and teachings.

Jenny, Krista, and Olga, for their gracious support and many wonderful cups of chai tea.

May the merits of this book be of benefit to them.

In keeping with the tradition of anonymity and confidentiality in the Twelve Step program, names of people mentioned in this book have been changed, along with details that would identify them.

1

Joining the Great We

Step One | We admitted we were powerless over alcohol—that our lives had become unmanageable.

I WOKE UP in the isolation ward.

Doctor Schultz, tall, lean, and wrinkled with time, squinted through thick glasses. When he treated my grandmother, he used to make house calls. Now, he poked and prodded with gloved hands, head to toe in surgical blue, grunting monosyllabic comments.

"What's wrong with me?" I asked.

"You are very ill."

"Can you make me better?"

"I'm trying."

The initial diagnosis was spinal meningitis, and the treatment was several days lying on a bed of ice to lower the 104-degree fever. Later, the diagnosis was revised to a severe case of mononucleosis. The old-school Doctor Schultz never asked if I had run myself into the ground by using drugs, and I didn't whisper a word. Not until week four of the hospital stay did it inkle through my mind, *Could it be that I collapsed because of taking all that speed?*

1

The moment of awareness stands still in time. Two years and then some of nearly daily use, popping white crosses and other street junk to keep going, working three jobs to make grades and tuition and rent. I went to a private college I didn't want to go to, kept up a high grade-point average because I had to. My father expected no less. But amphetamines erased all limitations. I could do anything, never had to sleep, was the life of the party. It was marvelous, magnificent, drug-induced bliss.

Doctor Schultz told me to take a semester off from college. He said I had to put some weight back on, get eight hours of sleep every night, and take vitamins. I was burned out at twenty-two years old. I didn't want to stop using, but I was scared of dying. On the other hand, it wasn't exactly like I wanted to live.

My girlfriend's guy friend, Skip, went to Alcoholics Anonymous (AA) meetings. I asked him what he thought I should do. He said maybe meet up with him at AA sometime; most people stop their drug use before they end up in the hospital for a month, their health in shambles.

I said I'd think about it.

I LOVED THAT GOLD CAMARO but the tires were jinxed. They slid on the black ice hidden beneath the snow, bumping the curbside and blowing a tire. The cold weakened the seal, leaking air. Even the new radial tires didn't help. It was the sixth flat tire so far that year, and it was still cold as a bitch. Bummer. If not for that tire, I might have sat in front of the church for a while and then driven away. But I had to go in and ask for help to put on the spare. The bitter windchill made my hands too stiff to manage it alone.

Saint Matt's Episcopal Church is on the north side of Lake of the Isles, warm and bright and hung with colored lights. "'Tis the season," December 27, 1975. The sting of cigarette smoke hits as I walk in, hazy, stinky air. Voices jingling with laughter, underscored by raspy, hacking smokers' coughs. A stranger comes up, right hand extended.

"Hi, are you new? Is it your first time here? Grab a cup of java over there by the kitchen window."

Friendly, happy people are hugging and slapping each other on the back. Lots of friendly, happy people. *What the hell is wrong with them?* But it's kind of nice, comforting. Maybe I will stay for the meeting after all.

There's the little flat tire problem to deal with. Skip said he'd meet me here, and I don't want to stand him up.

Six months after my health breakdown, I'd made it to my first Twelve Step meeting of Alcoholics Anonymous.

I kept going, at first because hanging with people and having coffee after the meeting was fun. And I loved the anonymous part of the meetings. Nobody had to know anything about me. I was safe. I could just come in, sit down, and belong. People were accepting, encouraging, and inspiring. They weren't the losers I thought they would be. It was surprising, unsettling really, to hear people talk openly about their struggles and fears. I had a place with this group of other misfits.

I kept coming back, hoping it would somehow do some good, yearning for the serenity others seemed to have. I wanted to change but didn't know how. People didn't change in my family.

I COME FROM, I NOW KNOW, generations of Irish alcoholics. At least four generations of alcoholics, way back to the "old country." On my first visit to Ireland, when I was piecing together my family tree for a project in graduate school, I tracked down my father's second cousins. I learned that dear old Grandpa didn't come to the United States because of the potato famine after all. He was in trouble with the law, sloppy drunk and knocking over gravestones, getting into brawls at the pubs. He fled the country, bringing his temper with him. His father before him was an alcoholic. Half the family in the old country was alcoholic. Half the family in this country is alcoholic.

And there it is: a whole painful, lonely, shame-based, violent family tree. "We" meant being doomed—genetically wired to self-destruct. Walking into that first meeting was an admission that I needed help, couldn't do it alone anymore. Had there been any other way, I would have passed.

Now, thirty-five years later, I owe the programs of Alcoholics Anonymous and Al-Anon my life. I've stayed straight and can say I am genuinely happy. My wake-up call at the age of twenty-two was a life-changing "failure." The migraines, ulcerative colitis, and dependency on pills are gone. I confess that abstinence from drugs, in and of itself, was not all that difficult. The much harder part has been learning how to live sober.

The Twelve Step program opened access to an inner spiritual life—a part of me sealed shut, bitter and hard from my Catholic upbringing. After several years in recovery, I became keenly interested in mindfulness and meditation. By chance, I read Lillian Roth's biography, *I'll Cry Tomorrow,* the story of her decline and recovery from alcoholism. She mentions an Inter-Group pamphlet published in the 1950s, which outlined similarities between the Twelve Steps and a set of contemplative practices from the sixteenth century, the Ignatian Exercises. These are a set of prayers, visualizations, and "thought experiments" to be carried out in a retreat setting under the guidance of a spiritual director. The exercises are based on the experiences of Saint Ignatius of Loyola, who offered them as a way to discover God's will and carry it out in our daily lives. I had never heard of them, despite decades of Catholic education. None of my friends in the program had heard of them either.

Eventually I discovered the Cenacle House in Wayzata, Minnesota, a local contemplative center offering a yearlong retreat on the Ignatian Exercises. I signed up in an instant, motivated by what I thought was sheer curiosity. I think now there might have been something more to it, perhaps a deep thirst, a need to find lasting happiness.

The Ignatian retreat started a spiritual journey that has taken me to many places and has inspired practice and study with many people. I continued to train at the Cenacle House during the next ten years, gaining a certificate in spiritual direction. Also, I was interested in Eastern contemplative practices and traveled to study meditation in India, Nepal, and Zen Buddhist monasteries in the United States. I completed graduate studies in psychology and became licensed to practice as a psychotherapist.

These threads, together with the Twelve Steps, wove my recovery from drug dependency and helped mend the effects of growing up in a violent, chaotic, alcoholic family.

Four Pure Insights

In recovery, I grappled with the reality of suffering, the thing I hated about life and sought to escape with drug use. I wondered: What's wrong with me? How did I end up addicted to drugs, despite never wanting to be like my alcoholic father? Why do I hurt so bad and feel like I have a hole in my heart that will never heal?

In meditation classes I was introduced to the Four Pure Insights into the Way Things Are, a Buddhist teaching that shed light on these questions.[1] Sometimes called the Four Noble Truths, the text became an important source of comfort and relief in my recovery.

Four Pure Insights into the Way Things Are, among Gautama Buddha's earliest teachings, were given shortly after his monumental awakening under a bodhi tree. He had spent his entire adult life roaming the countryside, trying to come to grips with the reality of suffering in the world. He abandoned his family's wealth, kept no earthly possessions, fasted, meditated, and pursued understanding truth. Once enlightened, the Buddha taught about four principal realities of suffering.

The First Insight: Suffering

The first insight is that suffering is an intrinsic part of life. (The Pali word for suffering is *dukkha*, translated as a "thirst" or "unsatisfactoriness" that does not go away.) Life serves it up in one form or another. Dukkha isn't anybody's fault. It just is. Attempting to push away or control the uncontrollable is folly.

In hearing this insight, I have an image of the Buddha looking and sounding like a counselor from the PharmHouse treatment center in the 1970s, in plaid shirt, torn blue jeans, and a long ponytail, saying "So, deal with it!"

We face the truth of Gautama Buddha's first teaching in the First Step of the Twelve Step program, admitting we are powerless over alcohol (and alcoholics)—that denying and trying to manage our addictive mind is unmanageable. Buddha says this too: dukkha, or thirst, is inexhaustible. For Twelve Steppers, our dukkha is addiction and codependency. For others it may come in other forms, such as change, illness, loss, or death. But it comes.

The Second Insight: Our Response to Suffering

The second reality, or "truth," is that we have an internal response to the dukkha we encounter. For every external event that arises, we have an internal reaction that co-arises. Some of our reactions cause or compound the suffering already there. Examples include numbing out with drugs or alcohol, blaming ourselves or others, and trying to manage and control another person. We have our own personal brand of insanity, alive and well and inside of us, not "done to us" by others.

Buddha, like the founders of the Twelve Step program of recovery, encourages rigorous personal honesty and self-observation. He taught practices of mindfulness meditation to develop greater self-knowledge and self-control.

The Third Insight: Transforming Our Response

Third, we aren't doomed or stuck; we don't have to keep on suffering. Buddha says it is possible to transform our internal responses to the outside events we cannot control. Western neuroscience has confirmed this noble truth, showing in before-and-after brain scans that an ongoing practice of mindfulness and loving kindness meditation changes our brain chemistry and activates our left prefrontal lobe, the brain's "happiness center."[2] If we are willing to deeply engage in spiritual practice, we will change, even down to the cellular level.

The Fourth Insight: A Path to Transformation

The final insight is that there is a path out of suffering. The concrete practices of mindfulness, loving kindness meditations, and ethical living open the way to a life of greater peace and happiness.[3] The Twelve Step recovery program gives us specific steps to follow, practices that are amazingly similar, in spirit if not in language, to those of Buddhism.

Further, the Buddha says it is noble to stay with our human experience of suffering. Through it we connect with the all other beings, a great joy.

What? Usually, suffering shrinks our world, occupied only by me and my misery, thank-you-very-much. When dukkhas ("thirsts") such as loneliness, addictive cravings, or angry feelings take hold, we get lost in our own bubble of pain and separateness. Buddha's insight was that believing we are unique and alone is a basic human delusion.

Releasing the Delusion of Separateness

The double life of my addiction created a wall between me and others. Between the ages of sixteen and twenty-two, I used regularly, but secretly, and was proud of it. I maintained an honor-roll grade-point average, never missed a payment for my Camaro, and worked three part-time jobs to pay my college tuition. (Okay, so I was late to work a few times. Maybe more than a few times. Maybe I didn't show up once in a while . . .) Outside, solid citizen. Inside, jumbled-up head case. Ulcerative colitis, migraine headaches, anxiety, and a closet amphetamine user. No one had a clue until I broke down and landed in the hospital. It had been a quiet, hidden path of utter self-destruction.

When I heard the First Step of Alcoholics Anonymous, "We admitted we were powerless over alcohol [and drugs]—that our lives had become unmanageable," the *we* word was like the sound of a foreign tongue. Strange. Unfamiliar. Like a pungent, tart lemon drop: your eyes water from the sour taste. Then you want another one. Although I recoiled from the idea of being part of a "we," I yearned for it too.

In Twelve Step meetings, I was surprised to hear how many others felt cut off and alone too. Even the delusion of separateness is a shared delusion. Tenshin-roshi Reb Anderson, senior dharma teacher at San Francisco Zen Center, says it like this: "You think that everybody's in the whole big world out there, and then there's this little separate bump over here and that's you."[4]

I first heard him talk about this nearly fifteen years ago. At that time I thought, "You bet that's the way it is. No doubt about it." In my family, I felt not only separate but more grown-up than my parents.

WE, MEANING MY SISTERS AND ME, were attempting to get my father recommitted for alcohol treatment. It would be the eleventh time.

My younger sister, Anne, called in the middle of the night, sobbing in fear and anger. "He's pounding on the door, hollering and swearing at me. The lock is going to give. Mother is in bed with a headache."

The usual story. She was in danger; he would hurt her. He was violent when he was drunk, funny and charming when sober. A pillar of the church community.

"Crawl out the window and run to the corner of the block, next to the Sims's house," I said. "Bring your clothes and stuff for school. Watch for my gold Camaro. I'll be there to pick you up in about thirty minutes. Don't try to talk Mother into coming with you. Just leave."

I lived in an apartment by Lake Calhoun with my sister Cecile, two years my senior, both of us under twenty. That weekend, as the three of us talked, we decided it had to be done. Our plan was to call the social worker in charge of his case and sign papers to have the court send my father back to Anoka State Hospital. It was a wrenching decision.

Anoka State Hospital stunk with all the crazies peeing in their pants and not enough staff to take care of them. The food was gross. The court had sent Dad there for his tenth treatment, because he was violent, had threatened us, and then tried to kill himself with his gun. The judge could bounce him back in with the stroke of a pen. We all three swore to stand together, no matter how tough it got.

After a few days, Anne insisted on going back home. She wanted to sleep in her own bed, see her friends at school. She promised not to tell Mom what we were planning. Once the judge signed the papers, the sheriff's department would "escort" my father to the hospital. No doubt it would be another ugly scene. Last time they dragged him away in a straitjacket, hollering like a wounded wolf. All the neighbors heard, I'm sure.

The following Friday afternoon the social worker called. Cecile had chickened out, refused to sign the commitment papers. Anne was legally still a minor, so I was it. The woman informed me that no one was home when the sheriff arrived at my parents' home that morning. I would later find out that Anne, feeling bad for Dad and scared of the possible repercussions of our plan, had spilled the works. My mother drove my father to Canada for the weekend to escape.

The social worker enunciated slowly, each word firm and to the point: "I don't think there is anything more you can do. It's obvious your father doesn't want to get treatment, your mother's enabling him, and your sisters do not agree with what you are doing. You need to give it up. *Get a life.* Go to Al-Anon."

I hung up, numb. Then I lay on the floor of the living room, unable to get up—cocooned in despair, alone, a bump on the side of the road while the rest of life passed by.

Admitting Our Suffering, Opening to Community

Perhaps many of us have dragged ourselves through the door of our first Twelve Step meeting, frustrated, impotent to change the addicts or alcoholics we love, admitting by our very presence that going it alone had failed us. Humiliated, perhaps, to let our hurt show, or to disclose we are out of control—powerless to handle our own drug or alcohol use, powerless to cure our alcoholic loved ones, powerless to manage others in any way. Striving for perfection, hiding our real self from others, or putting on a false face keeps us separate and alone.

But in the act of admitting our pain and suffering, we open up to a community. When we admit our failures, weaknesses, hurts, and needs, we find out we are not alone. A portal to connecting with others is opened.

Thích Nhất Hanh—a Vietnamese monk and, I believe, a holy person on this earth—describes it this way: "We have to recognize and acknowledge the presence of suffering and touch it. Please don't run away from suffering. Embrace it and cherish it. To do so, we need the help of friends in the practice."[5]

A fundamental teaching of mindfulness and Buddhism is that we are interconnected with all beings, all life forces. Believing we are separate, that I do not affect you and you do not affect me, is a delusion.

This is depicted in the story of Gautama Buddha's moment of enlightenment, which goes something like this: Gautama is sitting under a beautiful bodhi tree, meditating and maybe chanting "Ohm" after years of wandering, searching, and nearly starving to death. He is wrestling with his inner demons, watching them torture his mind. He touches the ground with his fingers, and as he does, the earth rumbles, rising to meet him. All of his suffering and distress falls away. In that moment he is awakened. He avows, "I, together with the great earth and all living beings, attain the way at the same time."

Buddha's enlightenment happens in concert with all beings, not alone. He declares his understanding that we are part of the "Great We," alive in a world of "interbeing," meaning that our existence is a shared experience. When we walk into a Twelve Step meeting and take Step One, we, too, touch the ground and experience the fellowship there to meet us. Realizing we are no longer separate and on our own, the veil of delusion is torn open.

Twelve Steps and Twelve Traditions (also known as the *Twelve by Twelve*) is the core text of Alcoholics Anonymous. It describes the experience of joining the Twelve Step community like this: "Through it we begin to learn right relationships with people who understand us; we don't have to be alone anymore."[6]

Even by myself in my room, I'm part of the Twelve Step fellowship. When I sit in mindfulness meditation, noticing breath, the texture of the cushion, and the sounds of the room, I begin by thinking about being part of the Great We.

Entering the Field in the Fellowship of Others

Tenshin-roshi Reb Anderson asked us to imagine ourselves in a great field with all of the buddhas and bodhisattvas (enlightened beings and spiritual seekers) that have come before us. The picture that popped into my mind was one of a giant football field, an expanse of meditators filling every inch. I imagined that I was surrounded by beings who understood my suffering and shared in my joys.

I never sat in meditation alone again. I started visualizing the "football field" filled with all kinds of people, ancestors, and practitioners going back to the time of Buddha, all meditating together. They breathed *in* as I breathed *in;* they breathed *out* as I breathed *out.* I could almost hear them chanting softly in my mind, the air filled with the scent of cedar incense. It was soothing, sweet. My body began to unwind, release. I was held in their grace.

Thích Nhất Hanh says he imagines all kinds of spiritual beings, even spiritual superstars, sitting in the great field with him when he meditates. Even though he is a Buddhist practitioner, he sees Jesus, Mother Mary, Martin Luther King Jr., and Mother Teresa. He has photos of each of them on the altar next to his meditation cushion. His grandfather is there on the altar, and other good friends.

This sparked me to call to my maternal grandmother and imagine her sitting in the field. I can see her face, smell the lavender scent of her perfume. She was big and plump, and I felt safe in her arms. I would run away to her house when things got really bad at home. When I imagine her sitting in the field, I can sense her smiling at me with a twinkling grin.

Now there are many more people from the here-and-now in the field. One is Jim, my husband of thirty years and dearest friend. I see his gentle, tender, wise face. I feel the presence of my sister Anne and the warmth of her generous, giving nature. My stepchildren, who have taught me how to love in ways I didn't know were possible, are also present. I recognize that they are my teachers. And there are the smiling faces of my granddaughters, Grace, Julia, and Olivia. I hear their giggles, sense the lightness of their innocent hearts. They helped me remember joy. Friends in sobriety are there, people who have become family, models of honesty and courage. There are many others.

The pain of admitting our failures and the unmanageability of what the world gives us opens the door to joining the Great We. I entered it at the moment of walking into Saint Matthew's Church, numbed from the cold, enfolded by warmth and the sound of laughter. There are hundreds and thousands of recovering people, in the past and in the present, all holding us in their kindness. There is no separation. We are them and they are us. Gradually, the sense of being separate has fallen away. This is a fruit of the Twelve Step fellowship, and an awakening that deepens with the practice of mindfulness and meditation.

Mindfulness Practice for Step One: Resting in the Field of Awakened Ones

When we are mindful that we share both the suffering and grace of others, we can face what seems unbearable. By opening our hearts, admitting our powerlessness over alcohol, drugs, and other people's choices, we are able to remember we are part of the great stream of We. If we let our mind rest for a moment or two (meditation), there is space for this awareness to arise.

Try this:

> *Take a few minutes to sit, be quiet, and rest the mind.* Just rest, and let yourself notice whatever is passing through your mind without doing anything about it. Just rest . . . relax with whatever arises.[7] Notice what it's like to breathe *in* and

breathe *out* . . . Just rest . . . Observe your thoughts, feelings, or sensations as they arise and pass through . . . letting them be . . . watching them pass through.

After a few moments of sitting with your breath in this way, place yourself in a great, expansive field with all the most loving people you've ever known or wish to know, surrounding you. All the enlightened people of old are sitting with you in this field, great buddhas and meditation practitioners. Imagine there is no separation of time and space, with all the energy and strength of those beings breathing with you, in each breath.

Call upon any of the buddhas, past or present, for help.[8] Maybe you would even say, "Grandmother, grandmother, I am here . . . right here . . . remember me?" In your own way, let yourself see these benefactors in your mind's eye, or sense the warmth of their kindness, or notice the sweet fragrance of their presence.

Now imagine you are part of a great stream of recovering alcoholics and addicts, members of the Twelve Step program, through seven generations in the past and seven generations in the future. Follow the cascade of anonymous faces, anonymous stories through many generations. Sense their understanding of your struggles, their ability to know what it's like inside your skin. Allow the strength of their recovery to hold you up, to support you like the cushion or chair you are sitting upon.

If you wish, in your mind, call to someone in the present: a loving person in your life, your sponsor, or a person who attends your Twelve Step meeting. Imagine this person's response of recognition and kindness. Allow yourself to feel your connection to him or her, and to all enlightened beings past and present, through all of time. Draw in the strength and wisdom of these beings, joining the Great We with each breath in, and each breath out.

❖ ❖ ❖

Continue this meditation for several minutes, one or two breaths longer than you think you can stand. In a pinch, you can use the short version from Thích Nhất Hanh: "I am not alone. Thank you."

2

Coming To

HOPE CAME TO ME in the guise of failure.

If it was Friday night, it was Mrs. Paul's frozen fish sticks for dinner. On Saturday, Swanson chicken pot pie. By the time I turned ten, I could heat them up in the oven, preparing dinner for my younger brother and sister. Mom and Dad ate out, usually at the American Legion or the VFW Post, because Dad said they had excellent steaks, grilled just right. Translation: They serve liquor. Lots of it. Cheap.

I'd go to sleep with half an ear on alert for their return, restless. I could hear them arguing out on the driveway, as soon as the engine shut down. The more he drank, the louder it got, with him swearing, slamming the cupboards, smashing the dining room chairs, and shattering Mom's curios against the wall. I had seen him punch my mother in the stomach and pull my sister Cecile's hair until she screamed for him to stop.

I knew all the places he hid his bottles: behind the draperies in the living room, between bottles of mouthwash in the back of the bathroom closet, inside his shoeshine kit in the basement. On Sunday mornings while he was still asleep, I'd sneak around, search out the bottles, and dump the booze down the drain of the laundry tubs. He never said a word. I bet he didn't even remember where he stashed his bottles.

I hated the fighting, hated him, and hated hating him. It didn't matter how many times we begged, pleaded, or called the cops. Nothing made any difference. He didn't stop drinking, hollering, or bullying; he was still the army sergeant barking orders. Only we weren't the inductees of decades past. We were his kids.

My sister Cecile ran away, got the hell out of there. She went to the nuns' house, the Sisters of Saint Joseph of Carondelet. They taught at our high school. Sister Ignatius came over to our house to tell my parents that Cecile was there; she told my father he should stop drinking, go to AA or something. I know because I eavesdropped from behind the door. He wasn't going to stop drinking, and my mother was never going to leave him either. She didn't have the backbone to do it, to raise four kids by herself. Besides, she was taking "tranqs" herself to cope.

When my mother cried, I tried to be good to make her feel better. I tried to take care of my younger brother and sister too. Anne and I made a nest behind the thick winter coats hanging in the spare closet. It was a great hiding place, but kind of cramped. At other times, we were just mean to each other, pent up with anger and helplessness.

Holidays were the worst. On Christmas Eve 1967, the arguing finally stopped around midnight. Wrung out, my parents slept. I didn't. I couldn't stand it anymore. Maybe I was despairing because holidays were supposed to be jolly and gay. Or maybe it was because Cecile was away at school and that left me "in charge" of the little kids, Joey and Anne. Just me, like I knew what to do. Not.

Maybe I thought *something* needed to wake up my parents, get them to stop the yelling and hitting. I was thirteen, old enough to know the arguments were out of whack. None of my friends' parents acted like mine. I felt trapped, locked in a cage. I had to get out.

It must have been late because everything was quiet, inside and out. No sounds of traffic from the street outside my window. I tiptoed out to the kitchen, straining not to make a sound. It would be hell if they woke up. I unlocked my mother's pillbox and took out three bottles. The green "pep pills," the yellow "nerve pills," and the white ones for her headaches.

That should do it. Hah. Maybe they'll feel bad too. I swallowed them down with two bottles of Coke. *Yes! Screw this miserable life. I'll show them. They'll be sorry when I'm dead.*

I lay on the bed as the room swayed back and forth, a skiff on a rolling lake. The Beatles posters bled together and dripped down the wall. My mind sank into a sweet quiet, drifting. Stillness wrapping me in its blanket.

Sometime or another I sensed a faint presence sitting on the edge of the bed. It was near, but nothing that could be grasped, like feathered kisses. It was sad. For me. Sad I wanted to die. Sad I had taken all those pills. I didn't want it to leave.

I don't know if I called to my mother or she just woke up, but she came into my room. Shook me and called my name, she said later. She saw the empty pill bottles by the bed and screamed at my father to get the car. Fairview Southdale Hospital was five minutes away.

After the doctors pumped my stomach, I was drowsy and sore, but alert enough to smell and hear the hospital all around me. Beeps and groans, rubbing alcohol and iodine. I could hear the emergency room doctor talking to my father on the other side of the curtain. "I'm going to discharge your daughter, but you need to take her to a psychiatrist. She needs help."

Oh, great. But later, my father told me he was going to do me a big favor and not make me go to the psychiatrist. No one in my family ever spoke of it again.

Many years later, I brought it up with my therapist. I told her that maybe an angel had wanted me to live.

She wanted to know what difference the angel's presence had made. I said, "It's why I'm not dead. I was touched by the kindness. I had a glimmer of believing I could get out of my family by another way. By getting well."

Seeing Our Internal Response to Events

Eight years after that Christmas Eve overdose, I found the Twelve Step program and started on the path to recovery.

In the interim, I was a depressed and lonely teenager. I medicated my pain with drugs, from popping my mother's prescription Valium, to smoking dope and cigarettes, to taking amphetamines and junk from the street. All in secret. It was the slower suicide route.

But, in the back of my mind, I sensed there had to be a better way to live. The touch of the angel had left its imprint. After I turned twenty-two and my health crashed, I reached out for recovery—something no one in all generations of my family had ever done. In the past, we Stewarts just died from alcoholism.

When I walked into that first AA meeting, thirty-some years ago, it was a decision to *try* living. I was still highly ambivalent, the addict part of me wanting to run away. Others in the program spoke about enthusiasm, gratitude, and joy, but in those early days I often thought, *I'll just take "standing it," okay? Forget joy. That would be asking for too much.*

How do we learn to stand it? To accept our own and others' flaws and not be angry, hurt, lonely, or ashamed much of the time? To have hope we can be restored to sanity? Here, in this life? If *dukkha* is inescapable, as the first of the Four Pure Insights into the Way Things Are says—if greed, anger, and ignorance arise endlessly[2]—then what do we do? How can we learn to stand difficult and painful emotions with a peaceful heart?

The second Pure Insight into the Way Things Are helps with these questions. It says that for every external event or situation life brings us, we have an internal response. *It is the combination of the two that causes our suffering.*

Buddhist philosophy calls this phenomenon *dependent co-arising.* (With a slip of the tongue, I've sometimes said "codependent arising.") If part of the suffering equation is our own mental and emotional reaction, it follows that we would suffer less if we could change that reaction for the better. Great! We can do something.

New breakthroughs in Western brain research tell us that it is possible to rewire our emotional patterns at a neurological level.[3] New emotional habits etch new neural pathways in the brain, something other than the old responses of seeking escape, blaming ourselves or others, and looking for love from external sources such as other people or material things. Maybe we *can* be restored to sanity.

In my mind, I can still hear the voice of a member of Al-Anon. He said, "You can be happy in spite of your family. You don't have to go down with them."

What? Are you nuts? You mean even if my family is wrapped up in a life of violence, alcohol, and self-destruction, I can still be happy? I don't need to get high to stand the pain? <u>I can choose a different way of being in the</u> <u>world</u>? With at least four generations (that I know of) of Irish alcoholics and their codependent counterparts in my family, it seemed like he was saying I could reverse the force of gravity.

ON A SATURDAY AFTERNOON IN NOVEMBER 1983, a relative called unexpectedly. Her voice choked as she told me that her husband had pushed her out of their moving car the night before. He was torqued-up on liquor and, she suspected, other hard drugs. It wasn't the first time their arguments had escalated into violence.

"Please," she said, "You're a counselor. What should I do? Can't you talk to him?"

"Go to Al-Anon. This is just what my father was like, and it's awful. Don't live with violence and the fear of it. Go to Al-Anon. Get counseling."

That night I wrote a long letter to her husband. I told him I was concerned, pleaded with him not to continue the cycle of violence, and said I hoped he would seek help. I told him that Twelve Steps, meditation, and therapy had helped me, that I wasn't as depressed or self-destructive as I used to be.

He called a few days after he received the letter. He was seething in anger, his voice hard, telling me that I was butting into his business. (True.) He said to keep my nose out of his affairs. He didn't speak to me for twenty years.

As usual, I racked my brain trying to figure out what I had done wrong. Why was he treating me like this? What was so bad in the letter? I had shown it to several people, gotten feedback, before I sent it, and I felt good about it. <u>But I went into a tailspin of self-doubt, fear, and shame—a</u> <u>full-fledged codependency</u> attack. <u>Insanity</u> had me <u>by the tail</u>.

Years later, however, I heard from him again. He thought he recognized himself in one of the stories I included in my first book, *Paths Are Made by Walking*. His response was a scathing, threatening, nasty-gram via e-mail.

<u>This time</u>, there was <u>no tailspin</u> of self-doubt. I just wanted off the <u>merry-go-round of insanity</u> and violence. I replied that I was sorry he was unhappy with the book, but I would receive no more raging, threatening e-mails. <u>With a mixture of sorrow and relief, I blocked him from my elec-</u> <u>tronic address book.</u>

There have been successive moments of clarity in my recovery. Awakenings. Moments when the mind is calm enough to see things as they really are.

So often, as with my father, I come face to face with being powerless over another person's choices. I am not responsible for others' actions—their threats, alcohol use, or violence. Using drugs to escape the pain of a relationship and the shared history of our family was my own insanity. Sometimes darkness gives rise to dawn.

Awakened Beings Are Just like You and Me

Buddha, too, awakened. He stopped wandering and seeking something outside the life that is right here. His enlightenment did not occur because he was a supernatural being, unlike you and me. In fact, stories about him say he was quite human—with one important difference.

One day, soon after the Buddha's enlightenment, a man saw the Buddha walking toward him. The man had not heard of the Buddha, but he could see that there was something unique about the man who was approaching.

"Are you a god?"

The Buddha answered, "No."

"You're a magician, then? A sorcerer? A wizard?"

"No."

"Are you some kind of celestial being? An angel, perhaps?"

Again the Buddha said, "No."

"Well, then, what are you?"

The Buddha replied, "I am awake."[4]

We also wake up in Step Two of Alcoholics Anonymous: "Came to believe that a Power greater than ourselves could restore us to sanity." We "come to," out of the fog of our deluded, addictive mind, reaching for something more. There, waiting for us, are the ancient practices of meditation and mindfulness, practices that teach us how to "be enlightened rather than defeated by all the various situations of life."[5]

Although our path is called "recovery," it is essentially a spiritual path that many others, through eons of time, have also walked. As Steve Hagen explains in *Buddhism Plain and Simple:* "We call Gautama 'the Buddha,' but many other buddhas, many other awakened human beings, exist, and have existed. And every buddha—past, present, and future—is a human being, not a god."[6]

I thought of buddhas as holy and good, and in contrast thought of myself as defective and bad. It amazes me to think of enlightened people of old as being just like you and me. Even more astounding is to think we are interconnected to those very beings now, that we can share in their wisdom and access their compassion. The same awakening of kindness I felt sitting on the edge of the bed when I was trying to suicide my life away. Could there be angel dust in me?

Restored to Sanity by Touching Our "True Face"

Spiritual teacher Eihei Dōgen Zenji, thirteenth-century Japanese Soto Zen founder, describes how we are indeed part of this power greater than ourselves in his teaching "Lofty Ancestor Eihei Dōgen's Verse for Arousing the Vow":

> May [all buddhas and ancestors] share with us their compassion, which fills the boundless universe with the virtue of their enlightenment and teachings. Buddhas and ancestors of old were as we; we in the future shall be buddhas and ancestors . . . Because they extend their compassion to us freely and without limit, we are able to attain buddhahood and let go of the attainment.[7]

❖ ❖ ❖

Teachings such as Dōgen Zenji's are referred to as the "teachings of the awakened," or *buddha-dharma*.[8] They suggest the power to restore us to sanity is accessed by touching our own inner essence, one that we share with all beings and all of life. This inner essence is called our "true face," or "original nature," the buddha within. Even if we have forgotten it, even if it is tangled up with distorted beliefs and ideas we have learned about ourselves, this inner essence is still beautiful and good, present and within reach.

Perhaps it's easier to see it in other people. In a class here at Mind Roads

Meditation Center, we were talking about this teaching one afternoon, discussing the idea of our shared buddha nature. I asked people, "How would that affect how you live, if you imagined or believed that your true face was beautiful and good?"

In one small group, a delightful Peruvian woman—kind, educated, hardworking, and struggling with compulsive overeating—said, "Well, yeah, I believe that idea of everybody's got a buddha nature. Only, I just think that maybe I got passed over when they were handing it out."

I couldn't believe my ears. And I felt sadness, realizing she believed what she was saying. *Wait a minute,* I thought. *I felt like that too, for years.* At that moment, I realized I was thinking in past tense. I no longer felt that I had been passed over when buddha natures were doled out. Amazing!

Enlightened people of old were just like us. They probably screwed up too. They had self-doubt. Maybe some of them were even a little obsessive. Maybe their hope was born from failure, when they awakened to the reality of their insanity. How many came to believe, through experience, that a spiritual path could in fact lead them to happiness? Just like you and me. As a buddha of old once said in verse:

> WHEN I FINALLY REALIZED THE WAY,
> THE WHITE SNOW, WHICH HAD BLANKETED ALL
> IN A THOUSAND LAYERS, DEPARTED.[9]

❖ ❖ ❖

Accessing Our True Nature through a Still Mind

Mindfulness meditation helps us contact the inner essence of beauty and life. It offers a gateway to freedom from our habitual responses, liberation from the addictive mind.

The core practice of mindfulness is breath awareness meditation, called *zazen* in Japanese. We train our mind to stay in the moment, aware of the sensations of breathing, "feeling the body in the body."[10] At the end of our exhale, during the slight pause before the inhale—during the space between our busy thoughts—our true nature can arise.

A quieted, still mind allows access to the true nature within, opening a gateway for joy and gratitude to arise. It trains us to be less reactive to our inner thoughts and other people. Pema Chödrön, a Buddhist priest and one of the foremost teachers of loving kindness practices in the West, says the following four qualities are cultivated when we meditate:[11]

- *Steadfastness.* When we meditate, we practice listening to ourselves, staying with our arising thoughts and emotions. Instead of traveling the same old mental pathways of tuning out, escaping with drugs or alcohol, or running away from our emotions, we are cultivating being intimate and true to ourselves, in body as well as mind.

- *Clear seeing.* A calm mind fosters clear seeing, which is another way of saying that if we practice mindfulness, we will have less self-deception. We learn to be honest, and delusions fall away. When we sit in meditation, we observe our mind, watching the thoughts pass through, all the mental traffic honking, swerving, and cutting in. We practice holding "bare attention" toward the thoughts and feelings that arise, accepting them with kindness and nonjudgment.

- *Experience of our emotional distress.* During meditation, we don't try to make ourselves be anything other than what we are. We are open and curious about whatever arises, neither pushing our thoughts away nor clinging to them in morbid self-reflection. We drop the "story line," all the ways we are interpreting our distress signals, and just experience the pure energy of our fear or other emotions. Thus "we learn to abide in the experience of our emotional distress."[12]

- *Attention to the present moment.* During meditation, we make the choice, moment by moment, to be here in our life, one breath at a time. We welcome and pay attention to our mind and body, in itself a way of practicing kindness, "being tender toward self, toward other, and toward the world."[13]

Meditation takes us just as we are, with our joy, confusion, or insanity. We have a direct relationship with our being—not blurred by alcohol or chemicals, without looking to food or sex or drugs or money or anything outside ourselves for a happiness "fix." Rather, we face the reality of our lives, seeing that change is necessary. Coming to. Waking up.

Mindfulness Practice for Step Two: Prepare for Sitting

Mindfulness practice can restore us to sanity by training our responses to be calmer and more authentic. I encourage you to establish a sitting meditation practice at home. True, it's wonderful to calm ourselves when we sit for twenty minutes in a Twelve Steps and Mindfulness meeting, but the fruits of meditation really grow with regular practice. If you take time to sit—whether it's on a cushion or in a chair—without reading, without journaling, without thinking, it allows calmness to permeate your subconscious more deeply, breaking up old fears and healing crippling shame. There is no other way to receive the benefits. It takes doing, actually "putting time in on the cushion."

Try this:

> *Begin by noticing the sensations of the body sitting on the cushion or in the chair, taking a quick spot check on the body and the posture of sitting.* Notice your base and make any adjustments you need to so that your legs and feet are flat on the cushion or flat on the floor, sitting comfortably. Root that base of the body into the earth and notice the sensations of being supported by the cushion, the chair, the floor, and the earth beneath, all holding you up.
>
> *Now spot-check the root of the pelvis and let yourself rock slightly, if need be, to find a point of balance.* Distribute both sides of your weight equally on the cushion. If you're on a zafu (a small cushion that meditators often use), then make sure you are resting up on your sit bones to avoid having your legs fall asleep. The base of the body is now rooted and balanced.
>
> *Out of that balance, imagine that the spine can open space between the vertebrae, letting it stretch upward.* This opens a clear channel for breath so the prana, or life force, can flow

easily and clearly. It's out of this rooted balance that upright-
ness can arise.

Next, check the head. Balance the head so that it's neither
tilting forward nor leaning back, but so that the ears are lined
up with the shoulders. The jaw is even and relaxed—easy jaw.
Let the tongue roll up behind the upper teeth if that helps you
to keep the jaw loose.

Notice the hands. Let the hands be in an intentional
expression, or *mudrā.* If you are frightened, wishing for
greater solidness or strength, then rest your palms down on
top of your thighs for stability. If you are tense, wishing for
greater receptivity, sit with the palms facing upward on your
knees in a gesture of openness. If you want to remember
your oneness with the cosmos, with all beings, then let one
palm rest inside the other palm, facing upward and with
thumbs touching and wrists resting on the thighs, promot-
ing oneness with all that is.

Notice the eyes. Let your eyelids close themselves, all the way.
Or, if you are feeling tired or sloggy-minded, avoid falling
asleep by holding your eyes slightly open and fixed on a spot
on the floor or wall.

❖ ❖ ❖

Once you've lined up all these six points of posture, notice what it's like
to sit with the body in this mountain position.

Mindfulness Practice for Step Two:
Breathing and Noting Meditation

After you arrive in the sitting posture described in the previous practice,
stay as still as possible without undue pain or discomfort. Begin now to let
go of the small stuff—the body's itches and twitches. Practice not reacting
to them. A still body and a stable body cultivate calmness and serenity.

Try this:

Turn the mind toward noticing the breath. Let your attention
focus on the spot in your body that's easiest for you to feel the
breath. Notice the sensation of the inhale and a sensation of
release with the exhale. Ride the exhale all the way to the end,
noticing the slight pause right before the body fills itself,
allowing the *in*-breath to fill you without effort. There's no
need to make your breath do this or that; just let your body
breathe you, noticing how it feels.

If it steadies you, count the exhales. Count one with each
out-breath until you arrive at the number ten. Then begin
again.

*If you prefer, release the counting and just stay with aware-
ness of the breath and the body.* Begin to let all thoughts pass
through, just letting them arise and move on by. They are a
bit like the passing motion of traffic in the background—
whooshing, swishing, roaring, arising, and moving on. Just let
them pass on by, pass on through.

Notice when the mind wanders. This is its nature. The
moment you notice your mind wandering, note your distraction and go back to the breath. Call yourself back gently,
kindly, staying with this awareness of your own breath for
the next few moments.

❖ ❖ ❖

Do this for five to ten minutes at first, building your way up to twenty
to thirty minutes each day.[14]

3

Taking Refuge

| Step Three | We made a decision to turn our will and our lives over to the care of God *as we understood* *[God]*. |

THE "AWAKENED ONES" IN BUDDHISM tell us that despite the inevitability of suffering *(dukkha),* we are not trapped. There *is* a way out of suffering to greater peace. But the way out may not be what we imagine.

For me, getting out meant going in.

I began to learn about meditation and mindfulness when I was twenty-four years old, two years into my sobriety. We were eating tuna sandwiches with tomatoes and lettuce on thick slabs of whole grain bread at Professor Munchies on Hennepin Avenue. It was hard to get my mouth open wide enough to take a bite.

My friend Father Tim Power was describing a monastery he went to on retreat. He painted pictures of towering red rock and deep green, sweet-scented juniper pines surrounding a rich quiet and peace. Complete silence, no talking allowed. Six times a day, bells ring to call everyone to meditation. It was some kind of Christian-Zen hybrid, a contemplative community started by a Carmelite priest.

With a sandwich halfway to my mouth, I felt a fierce desire come up like a rush, refusing to be ignored, as if a magician had told me to turn into a chicken and all I could do was cluck. I *had* to go to that monastery, see it, and feel it for myself. It was called Nada, Spanish for "emptiness." The monastery rested in the foothills of the Spirit Mountains in Arizona, near Sedona, on old Hopi Indian worshipping grounds, land so majestic and beautiful it was sacred and used only for religious ceremonies.

I imagined a place of joy, simplicity, and peace. I was hoping for a much-needed natural high. Later I realized I was looking for a way to spiritually bypass my emotional pain and the difficulties of being here, in life. Present. I wanted to rise above it all, float on the clouds of spiritual bliss.

I was in for quite the surprise.

The monastery was a tired collection of hermitages sprinkled across acres of high desert cacti, red rock, and rolling, craggy brush. My dwelling was a one-room shack with a mattress on boards held up by two sawhorses, a bare wooden desk, hooks for clothes, and a one-burner hot plate. There was a small refrigerator in one corner, a toilet and sink in the other. We grew what we could in the huge garden, producing massive amounts of zucchini. The rest of our groceries came from the food shelf in Phoenix: peanut butter, cheese, rice, soup, and cartons of expired yogurt.

We talked only on Sundays after Mass, visiting and playing volleyball or flying kites on the rooftops of our hermitages until early afternoon. The rest of the time there was silence. We ate alone in our hermitages, did manual work in the morning, had study time for reading, writing, or walking in the afternoon. Bells rang six times a day for meditation, following the old Catholic tradition of Divine Office. The simplicity and routine of the eremitic schedule was soothing. All decisions about what to do were already made. All I had to do was give myself over to it.

The chapel was a round stone structure without windows, cool and dark and still, dug into the ground, like a Hopi kiva. On Saturdays there was an all-night vigil. Each of us signed up to meditate for one hour, from dusk until dawn. Being an as-yet-unreformed night owl, I signed up for the 2:00 to 3:00 a.m. shift. When the moon was full, its light was so bright I didn't even need my flashlight to walk from my hermitage to the chapel. Grand rock formations, twisted firs, and the stone-lined pathways were aglow in the dark. Shadows were exposed in the soft blue light of the moon.

After the first six months of routinely falling asleep in meditation, memories from childhood began to slosh around at the edges of my awareness. Fuzzy at first but gradually coming into focus. There were simply no distractions. No TV, no telephone, no computer, no talking. Only a once-a-week meeting with Father Michael, my spiritual director, and chitchat on Sundays. There was no place to run. Instead of an escape into bliss, I experienced a profound encounter with myself. Flashbacks to home as a girl and the feelings of fear, helplessness, and anger, anger, anger. The dark edges of my psyche, illumined.

In the past, I was overwhelmed by the intensity of my emotional pain. This time, the environment of the monastery held me in its arms with velvet silence, simple routines, and the friendly company of chipmunks at my door. After weeks of meeting each Friday with Father Michael, my body began to relax. Little by little I started to unwind. Until then, I hadn't noticed that my muscles were rigid, braced against life, waiting for the next bad thing to happen. I didn't know there was any other way to be.

With nowhere to go, I had to either tolerate my feelings or run away screaming. The process was to simply stay with my inner turmoil and breathe while my feelings wheedled or stormed. Sit on the meditation cushion and do nothing; let memories, thoughts, and feelings pass on through; be held in the support of the community, the practice of meditation, the great field of all the kind, meditating beings through time. Great holy beings, ordinary beings, beings of all faiths and traditions were there in my mind's eye.

As the logjam of repressed emotion and shame about my alcoholic family released, I discovered there was space for something else. The sweet smells of spring in the desert and the twittering birdie who visited my heritage in the early mornings, begging for bread crumbs. I had an inkling of tranquility. It wasn't ethereal, just a feeling of being safe and coming home to rest.

Step Three as Taking Refuge
in the "Three Gems"

An Eastern view of "turning our will and our lives over to the care of God *as we understand God*" is to *take refuge*. In Buddhism, there is a tradition of taking refuge when you begin the spiritual path of transformation in earnest. It is a decision to look to meditation training and practice as a "shelter from the rain of problems and pain of life."[1] For me, an addict in recovery and an adult child of an alcoholic family, this was a decision to surrender, to give up looking outside myself for happiness and running away from the difficulties life brings. These had been my refuges. I had followed in the tracks of my ancestors.

But there were other ancestors to follow. The practice of taking refuge has been an ongoing, straightforward practice in the Buddhist tradition for over twenty-five hundred years. We decide to *depend* on it for the solace we once sought through drugs and alcohol, to let it be the safe harbor we seek in strife or storm. We commit wholeheartedly, realizing "half measures availed us nothing."[2]

Taking refuge sounded scary to me, but comforting too. I heard the wise and kind Tenshin-roshi Reb Anderson talk about it during a meditation practice period at the Green Dragon Temple (Soryu-ji) in California. He seemed like a pretty happy guy, shaved head and all. He portrayed taking refuge as "flying back to our true home."[3] Flying is active; it starts with accelerating into a takeoff.

Like Step Three in Alcoholics Anonymous, taking refuge is active. We decide to let go of our delusions of control, and instead turn toward three specific spiritual practices. These practices are called the "Three Gems," or "Triple Treasure," in Buddhist literature.

- *Taking refuge in awakening (buddha).* The treasure of awakening is recognizing that within us is a spiritual essence. Buddha called this essence our "buddha nature." He taught that our inner nature can be awakened, leading us to see the path of light and beauty in the world.[4] *Alcoholics Anonymous,* known as the Big Book to members of that fellowship, says it this way: "We found the Great Reality deep down within us."[5] Taking refuge in *buddha* is a decision to wake up to our true self.

- *Taking refuge in the path of mindfulness, understanding, and love (dharma).* The second refuge holds the treasures of mindfulness, understanding, and love. Teachings about these practices and the truths they are based upon, such as Buddha's Four Pure Insights into the Way Things Are, are called *dharma*. We take refuge in the dharma when we decide to study *Alcoholics Anonymous* and other spiritual teachings, abandoning our addicted ways of "self-will run riot."

- *Taking refuge in community (sangha).* The third treasure is our relationships with others: our family, friends, and the fellowship of the Twelve Step community. We need to decide to trust in people again, because we need their help to fully recover from our addictions and codependency. *Twelve Steps and Twelve Traditions* explains this decision: "It became clear that if we ever were to feel emotionally secure among grown-up people, we would have to put our lives on a give-and-take basis; we would have to develop the sense of being in partnership or brotherhood with all those around us."[6]

Let's look at each of the refuges more deeply, considering their implication for recovery from addiction and codependency.

Taking Refuge in Awakening (Buddha)

God within

The first is taking refuge in awakening or resting in "what you really are." In this practice, we devote ourselves to realizing the true nature of the mind—the mind in me, not some other, different mind. This is the same mind we share with beings of old, people who Dōgen said were just like you and me before they were enlightened. This mind is called *tathagatagarbha* in Sanskrit, the language of the original Buddhist texts. Various translations refer to it as our "true nature," "enlightened essence," "natural mind," "original face," "realized mind," or "buddha nature."[7] When we take refuge in awakening, we rely on the truth that we, too, can realize our true mind.

In the throes of addiction or raving codependency, we surely lose contact with our true buddha nature. I believed that, really, I was defective; walked around with a feeling of shame in my bones. I came from a "bad" family. My father was often publicly drunk—wobbling legs, slurred speech, and an empty grin on his face. Everyone in the neighborhood, in Saint Richard's parish, and at the American Legion where he drank knew

I was "Joe's daughter." I made it worse by using drugs and driving my own health into the ground, a wreck by the age of twenty-two, afraid of being found out. These were the kinds of ideas I had about who I really was.

Taking refuge in awakening suggests that many of the self-critical or self-important beliefs we hold are simply overlays, clouding and distorting our conscious contact with the "mind in its fullness . . . obscuring the brilliant qualities of Buddha nature, or natural mind."[8] I think of a carnival, with a loud, neon-lit, mental fun house, filled with mirrors. First, you're fat. Then, you're thin. Then, you're tall. Then, you're short. In the fun house, we know it's a hoax, product of smoke and mirrors. When it's our own inner voice saying, *I'm obscenely fat, I'm grotesquely skinny,* or *I'm a neurotic loser,* we believe it's the truth.

Tenshin-roshi Reb Anderson says that "what you think you are is not all of what you are . . . What you are is already attained, always, every moment."[9] I remember listening to Tenshin-roshi talk, sitting in a crowd of retreatants. He's going on in his very insightful and entertaining way about this concept that who we really are is a being already perfectly attained.

It was gibberish to my ears. I thought, *Right . . . sure thing, Mr. Monk. Let me introduce you to some of the people I know, my own father for one, and then tell me they are already "attained." Climb inside my skin, experience this fear and self-doubt and loneliness. Does this feel like "already attained" to you? What kind of Kool-Aid do you drink?*

Tenshin-roshi was suggesting a wild change in outlook. I wondered, *What would that be like, to live as if I actually believed I had an essential essence that is fundamentally beautiful and true, already attained?* What if, instead, I assumed I am a good person who has used drugs, had a troubled family, and kept secrets, fearing exposure? But I know I'm capable of selfish, angry, and self-destructive behavior. I know I'm an addict.

However, taking refuge in our buddha nature doesn't mean we magically turn into a new holy person. Rather, the process is one of remembering our true nature, recognizing our original face. Wake up to what's been true all along. Tenshin-roshi says, "It's not something special about you that makes you a buddha [an awakened being]. It's simply being you that is buddha. It is not that you are a virtuous person, so virtuous that you're a buddha, but that you being you *is* virtue."[10]

I HAD AN EXPERIENCE OF SIMPLY BEING, a moment when all self-consciousness fell away, under heaven's canopy.

The sky opened wide over the red rocks and desert sand at Nada. There were no buildings but our small hermitages, no billboards, no cars. You could see clearly, in all directions.

Whenever I went walking, I always wore my sturdy Red Wing boots. They were made of tough brown leather, too thick to be pierced by a rattler's fang. Scorpions were no danger. I was safe to roam, exploring the gorges and hills. It was easy to lose track of time, not seeing another human for hours. Me and the butterflies and groundhogs.

I took to singing aloud, full tilt. No one but the lizards and juniper trees to hear. Off-key or on-key, no matter.

I used to do the same thing as I tramped the cornfields across the street from my childhood home. When I was six years old, the lean stalks of corn were my green giant friends. They were gentle, protecting me from burning in the glaring sun. The dirt smelled of dung and grasshoppers buzzed. I could get lost, be invisible and free.

Wandering in the world of corn-spirits, I made up child-songs, belting away in my own innocent world. Mother couldn't see me, but she could hear. She'd later say all she had to do was stick her head out the back door and listen for a while. Then she'd know where to look.

While meandering around the desert lands surrounding Nada, I felt safe and free. I found that child-self again. And so I sang.

One favorite pastime was "composing" various melodies for the Canticle of Mary. From Christian scripture, it is Mary's prayer expressing wonder at the news that she is with child. Just a regular, "lowly" person, she is awed to hear the news that her child is a great being, the Messiah-to-come. She says:

> MY SOUL PROCLAIMS
> THE GREATNESS OF THE LORD,
> MY SPIRIT REJOICES IN GOD, MY SAVIOR,
> FOR HE HAS LOOKED WITH FAVOR
> ON HIS LOWLY SERVANT.
> FROM THIS DAY FORWARD ALL GENERATIONS
> WILL CALL ME BLESSED.

(Luke 1:46–48)

I can't really explain why I was so drawn to Mary's canticle. I just kept singing it time and again, rolling it around in my mind, having it pop up like a bad Chevrolet commercial. It said to me she felt loved, honored even though she wasn't "worthy." I identified with the not worthy part. Still, Mary was chosen and blessed. Maybe being worthy wasn't all it was cracked up to be.

One late fall afternoon at Nada, I was walking and singing, kicking up dust with my Red Wings. Soggy gray clouds lined the horizon, backlit by a sinking sun. Wide strokes of golden pink stretched across the sky, touching the cosmos. Everything was illumined, held in a breath of time. I could see clearly.

The prickly cacti thorns, yellow and pink desert blooms, and scraggly sage were all part of the magnificence of creation. Tarantulas, diamondbacks, and buzzards too. None had earned their place through virtue or worthiness. Like Mary, it was their very being that made them blessed. Surely me too? I belonged to this great creation. For a moment, I remembered who I really am. I returned home, singing.

When we take refuge in buddha, we are not giving ourselves over to a power "out there," separate from ourselves. In a radical turnabout from our addictions, we decide to trust that our deep inner nature is beautiful and true. Chinese and Vietnamese practitioners use the phrase, "I go back and rely on the buddha in myself."[11] In Step Three, we choose to awaken our true self, opening to the light and beauty in us and the world.

Taking Refuge in the Path of Mindfulness, Understanding, and Love (Dharma)

How can we be true to our nature and access it in a direct way? This is the second refuge, the path of mindfulness. We decide to study and practice ways that can open conscious contact with our true nature and lead us to greater happiness. We rouse our drowsy, addictive mind with the bell of mindfulness. Yongey Mingyur Rinpoche says, "As long as we don't recognize our real nature, we suffer. When we realize our true nature, we become free from suffering . . . When you begin to recognize [your buddha self] you change, and the quality of your life changes as well. Things you never dreamed possible begin to happen."[12]

On a practical level for me, this required sitting down on a meditation cushion, becoming familiar with and observing the mind, even letting it rest. Meditation was one of the few ways, other than drugs, that I experienced relief from the critical, bitter, and shame-based thoughts constantly chattering inside my head. When I went to live at Nada monastery, I delved into studying and practicing mindfulness and meditation.

At first, I nodded off during nearly every meditation period. Gradually, after a number of months, the exhaustion of my now-amphetamine-free-but-still-full-speed-ahead busy life seemed to run its course. I was getting enough sleep because there was nothing else to do. No nightlife in the monastery! Only the symphony of nocturnal creatures, me, the crickets, owls, and coyotes howling at the moon.

As time went on, little by little, the meditation training began to take hold. My brain wasn't hazy with drugs anymore, but the underlying addictive mind was fierce. Several hours each day in meditation began to quell the ceaseless self-criticism and corresponding depression. This happens by resting the mind in bare awareness, without judging, pushing away, or chasing down our thoughts. I learned to welcome the whole range of feelings, perceptions, and sensations rather *act them out* or *act them in*. I learned to just let all the different thoughts be—nasty, sleepy, dreamy, or scared—and watch them pass through my mind.

As childhood memories thawed, rising from the frozen corners of my unconscious, I felt unsettled. I was troubled by my emotions, especially feelings of grief and anger at my alcoholic family. I had clutches of panic, afraid of being flooded by my feelings. I wanted to run away, escape somehow, anyhow. Learning to accept my painful emotions, to be able to notice my thoughts instead of believe my thoughts, was one of the biggest breakthroughs of my time at Nada. I didn't know then, because the research hadn't yet been done, that meditation was also changing the very chemistry of my brain.

Another avenue for cultivating mindfulness is through study and reflection. At the beginning of my sobriety, this consisted of going to Twelve Step meetings, listening to the stories of people successful in recovery, and reading *Alcoholics Anonymous*. Later, while at Nada monastery, I also explored the practices of Christian contemplatives and the traditions of Zen meditation. Living in the present moment, developing inner quietude, and holding a mindful eye toward oneself and the world was at the heart of both.

Teachings on mindfulness and Buddhist philosophy didn't contradict my Christian upbringing. Instead, Eastern wisdom opened new ways of seeing and understanding life. Mindfulness and meditation offered spiritual access without tripping over the ghosts of my childhood religion. Taking refuge in *dharma* does not mean signing up to believe a particular dogma. Rather, it is taking a breath, "return[ing] to your island of self . . . a safe place filled with warm sunlight, cool shade trees, and beautiful birds and flowers."[13] We can realize the same truth as the enlightened ones of old, our ancestors in the Twelve Step program, and other awakened beings. We choose to explore the same path, walk the same steps, and come to the same peace. We decide to study meditation, take the actions it suggests, and try the practices of the awakened ones for ourselves.

If we commit wholeheartedly, decide to give right effort, we are promised that "the teachings of awakening will come alive."[14] Many doors to transformation will open. We hold them close, study them, breathe them. Let them start to breathe us.

Taking Refuge in Community (Sangha)

In the languages of Pali and Sanskrit, fellowship and community is called *sangha.* When we take refuge in sangha, we decide to give relationships with others a chance. The venerable Thích Nhất Hạnh says, "When a sangha shines its light on our personal views, we see more clearly. In the sangha, we won't fall into negative habit patterns. Stick to your sangha. Take refuge in your sangha, and you'll have the wisdom and support you need."[15]

While at Nada, I found life as a monastic appealing; I even applied to be a novice with the community. I liked the silence, simplicity, and solitude. Not having to talk to people was great. I didn't trust them anyway. After several very long spiritual direction sessions with Father Michael, I decided that was precisely why I needed to leave Nada. I was good at silence; it was easy. What I didn't know how to do was have relationships with people. I decided it would be better to reenter the world and learn.

Beautiful Buddhist texts talk about sangha as a group of people living in harmony, "beings we turn to for support, encouragement, and teaching."[16] Sangha is refuge.

My life experience was quite different. I learned about relationships in my family of origin, which meant they were unsafe, cruel, disappointing, and scary. I walked through life holding my breath, waiting for the next explosion, betrayal, or loss. When people said nice things to me, expressed their care or affection, not much of their warmth got in. My heart was sealed off for protection and survival. Taking refuge in the sangha, for me, was a conscious choice to build relationships with people. I wasn't capable of feeling trust; I had to *decide* to trust.

The fellowship of the Twelve Step program was my first taste of a sangha-like community. I was accepted without judgment. People were kind and giving. We had a common purpose—staying sober and practicing the Twelve Step program, hoping for greater serenity. From those early days, when I went to meetings because I looked forward to going out for coffee afterward, my understanding of trust and fellowship gradually changed. I began to experience what Buddhist teachers meant when they said community brings "peace and happiness to life."[17] With love and understanding, my heart began to soften.

The community at Nada was a second experience of true sangha. We were a group of people on a common spiritual path. Together, we sat in meditation six times a day, pulled weeds in the vegetable garden, laundered the sheets of visiting retreatants, and suffered the desert heat. We shared a yearning for peace and the willingness to practice meditation "like our hair was on fire." (Old Buddhist wisdom holds that we should seek enlightenment with the same urgency that a person whose hair is on fire would seek water.) We greeted each other with silent bows, supported each other with kind intentions, and prayed for each other's well-being.

I thought a monastic community would surely be free from strife, idyllic. It wasn't. Conflict occurred amongst members of the Nada community too. How could people who never even talk have conflict with each other? How could there be internal politics, power struggles, and an "in-group" of favored students inside the monastery? The common denominator of life inside or outside the monastery was people.

In real life, relationships are complicated, often challenging. With the clear seeing that comes with meditation, I became aware of how often I absorbed the "vibes" of other people in the community. I could sense if they were happy, sad, angry, or hurt with my well-attuned antennae. They didn't need to say a word. I was more mindful of when my stomach knotted up or my chest tightened. As a child, I had learned well how to read my father's moods and anticipate when he was going to blow, so I could make myself scarce. Scanning for danger had become an automatic impulse.

Taking refuge in sangha is a decision to learn how to do relationships differently than we learned as children. Relationships are a profound crucible for personal growth. For people with addictive personalities, this often means learning to be less self-absorbed, more aware of our effect on others. For people with codependency difficulties, it may require developing boundaries, taking in and taking on less of other people's feelings, needs, or blame. Even now, when someone is angry with me, my stomach clutches. Thoughts like *What did I do wrong?* or *Why is he or she treating me like this?* pass through my mind. In days past, I would strike back, yell louder than the other person, or say nothing but work myself over later with self-criticism. Mindfulness has helped me to temper my responses, at least sometimes. Other times, I am aware after the fact that I need to make amends. Try again. Aim for progress, not perfection.

There is a telling Buddhist story about how mindfulness can help us be less reactive, get less "hooked" by difficult people, even those who are intentionally cruel. Here is a paraphrased rendition:

> There once was an Indian man whose wife loved to gush over the Buddha, praising his wisdom and speaking of him with great admiration and affection. Although he didn't mind at first, he soon tired of it, flooding with jealousy.
>
> He clomped off down the road, headed for a showdown with Buddha, all righteous with a full head of steam. He wanted to humiliate the Buddha, ask him a question he couldn't answer, hoping his wife would be disenchanted. He asked the Buddha, "What do we have to kill to be able to live happily and peacefully?" The Buddha's reply was simple but it touched the angry husband, transforming him in that moment. "To be able to live happily and peacefully," the

Buddha replied, "one has to kill anger, for anger itself kills happiness and peace."

The man thought about what the Buddha said and decided to become a monk and follow the Buddha's teachings. Eventually, he became an *arahat*.[18] When his younger brother heard about how his older brother was now a respected monk, he in turn became enraged and jealous.

He went and confronted the Buddha, spewing insults and acting abusively. When he had finished his tirade, the Buddha asked him, "If you offered some food to a guest who came to your house and the guest left without eating any of it, who would the food belong to?"

The younger brother considered the question and finally conceded that the food would belong to him, not the guest. The Buddha then said, "In the same way, I do not wish to accept your abuse, so the abuse belongs to you." The man realized his mistake and felt great respect for the Buddha because of the lesson he had taught him. He, too, decided to study and practice the path.

Other of Buddha's students remarked about how amazing it was that Buddha could stay so calm and inspire others to take refuge in him. The Buddha replied, "Because I do not answer wrong with wrong, many have come to take refuge in me."[19]

✧ ✧ ✧

Thorny relationships and difficult people are powerful teachers if only we dare say yes to the lesson. Taking refuge in sangha is a decision to be open to learning from others—difficult people, kind people, or wise people. Once we open our heart to sangha, we realize that we are not a separate bump off to the side of life. Rather, we are part of a whole web of interbeing—a state of connectedness. When we see this, something inexplicable happens. Community co-arises.

We take refuge in the community, the fellowship of other beings, because we realize that we can't do it alone. We invest in a sangha, deciding to let others help us, and rely on them to teach us how to love. And, as Tenshin-roshi Reb Anderson notes, "When you take refuge in and give your devotion to [a spiritual path], there is always a response. All buddhas and ancestors say, 'Welcome home. Glad to see you. We've been waiting.' Now the family is back together. It's a concert, not a solo performance."[20]

Mindfulness Practice for Step Three: Three Refuges Prayer

A few months before his death, the Buddha was still talking about the power of taking refuge and counseled, "Take refuge in yourselves, not in anything else. In you are *buddha, dharma,* and *sangha.* Don't look for things that are far away. Everything is in your own heart."[21] If we are safe in refuges of buddha, dharma, and sangha, we can throw ourselves completely into our everyday life, moment by moment, and show up for our appointment with life.

Mental recitation is a meditative technique that helps a particular attitude or intention take hold. The repetition develops new neuropathways in our brain. The thought becomes a habit in a process that's like an athlete rehearsing a particular stroke or a dancer practicing a certain step. With practice we find that even when difficulties arise, the refuges are right there in the front of our mind.

Following is a prayer I hold in mind; it's my own quick-note version of prose written by Thích Nhất Hanh. I repeat it often at the end of a sitting period, much like a Buddhist Serenity Prayer.[22]

Returning home, taking refuge
in the buddha in myself,
May I, together with all beings,
realize my true mind.

RETURNING HOME, TAKING REFUGE
IN THE DHARMA IN MYSELF,
MAY I, TOGETHER WITH ALL BEINGS,
PRACTICE THE WISDOM OF MINDFULNESS,
UNDERSTANDING, AND LOVE IN MY DAILY AFFAIRS.

RETURNING HOME, TAKING REFUGE
IN THE SANGHA IN MYSELF,
MAY I, TOGETHER WITH ALL BEINGS,
CREATE HARMONY WITH OTHERS.

I AM AWARE THAT THESE THREE GEMS
ARE WITHIN MY HEART,
I VOW TO REALIZE THEM.

(Slowly recite the lines of the Three Refuges Prayer three times.)[23]

❖ ❖ ❖

An even shorter version from Thích Nhất Hanh refers to the Buddha as the living source of understanding and compassion: "Buddha in me, I give up. You do it."

4

Entering the
Green Dragon's Cave

Step Four	We made a searching and fearless moral inventory of ourselves.

IN STEP FOUR we take a "searching and fearless moral inventory of ourselves," looking at exactly how, when, and where we have caused difficulties for ourselves and others. At one time, the mere mention of Step Four made my body temperature go up, hands get clammy, and stomach churn with dread. I wanted to run screaming from the room.

I COULD SEE SAINT RICHARD'S CHURCH and school through the picture window of our house once I was tall enough to stand tippy-toe and look over the sill. There were six Quonset huts sitting along the edge of the church parking lot—squatty red rectangles with corrugated tin roofs, like a row of defensive linemen baring their teeth. In the 1950s, there were too many kids for the Catholic school to hold, baby boomers galore. When I started the second grade in 1960, the huts were still being used, paint peeling but standing strong.

Sister Michael Thérèse towered nearly six feet tall, white wimple snuggling her scalp and chin, starched collar resting over her floor-length black gown like a bib. A rough-cut wooden rosary hung over her corded belt, jangling as she moved. It sounded a momentary alert before she pinched an errant's ear or confiscated the treasured marbles that should have been left at home. All day we speculated about the color of her hair beneath the grand veil and searched for a loose strand to confirm our fantasies. Sister had the same name as me. How amazing. She was like an exotic bird, someone close to God who smelled like Ivory soap and had peppermint breath. I adored her.

A row of window transoms hugged the white ceiling tiles, sat along the seam where the sweltering tin roof met the institutional green walls. On warm days Sister would open the transoms, twisting a long metal extension rod that was difficult to maneuver. High up, the windows were hard to clean, and no shades blocked the sun's glare. In the spring, Sister was preparing us for our First Confession and First Communion, both scheduled for Palm Sunday, the week before Easter.

Sister was giving a lesson about sin. She pointed toward the window transoms with her ruler, saying, "Your soul is like that window, clear and light. Each time you sin, it makes a spot, like those flecks of dirt and dust, dirtying your soul. When you go to confession, it's like cleaning the window. Light can come through your soul again."

I thought I should confess as often as possible, because I didn't want my soul's window to be all spotted up with gunk. I wanted it to be clean.

Then Sister went to the blackboard and drew a picture of bottle.

"What is this, class?"

"A milk bottle, Sister."

"Yes! This bottle is like your soul. Pure and white and clean."

With a chunky stick of colored chalk in her hand, she started putting dots in the milk bottle. Just a few strokes at first, then more and more and more, until the chalk screeched in fury against the board. Sister gathered all her height, turning to face us with a fierce glare.

"*This* is what happens when you sin. Your milk bottle gets stained, *covered* with dark spots. You aren't good anymore. You *must . . . go . . . to confession.* It's the only way to remove the spots and become clean again. And, if you commit a mortal sin, your milk bottle is indelibly stained. There is no absolution. You are damned to hell."

I held my breath, stuck to the chair. My brain shorted out. Those black marks on the milk bottle sounded creepy. Big time. From then on, each time I thought or said or did something "wrong," I imagined stain after stain accumulating on my milk bottle.

I was scared all the time, excessively self-scrupulous. Everything I thought or did was analyzed and usually came up short. There were no mistakes, only failures and sins.

Years later, a psychologist gave me the word for this feeling—*shame*, a sense of being inherently deficient, indelibly stained.

Three Sources of Shame

The deep-seated shame of an addict or codependent makes it difficult to embark on a fearless and searching personal inventory. For me, a Catholic upbringing was only part of what shaped an identity steeped in shame. Other factors contributed too. In *Facing Shame: Families in Recovery,* Merle Fossum and Marilyn J. Mason state that there are actually three key influences that bring about a shame-based identity.[1]

We Can Inherit Shame from Our Family of Origin

This is where shame seeps in through our very pores, collecting from the unconscious of at least the three previous generations and passing through to us. We absorb the shame of family secrets, if there are some. These can include "no talk" items such as old crimes, violence, alcoholism, incest, bankruptcy, or childbirth out of wedlock. Any or all skeletons hidden in the cupboard qualify. We may or may not have heard the stories that garnered the shame, but we will surely feel its weight.

Shame can also arise from ethnic or cultural histories such as oppression or genocide. In my case, the influence of my Irish grandparents' legacy was profound. Monica McGoldrick, in *Ethnicity and Family Therapy,* says, "Many [Irish immigrants to the United States] wanted to forget the hundreds of years of English oppression they had endured and the desperate poverty they were fleeing."

Although my grandparents left the "old country" for a better life, they brought their shadow with them to the new land. McGoldrick says, "The Irish struggled with their sense of sin and guilt. Irish schizophrenics, for example, are commonly obsessed with sins they have not even committed. Basic to the Irish character is the belief that people are bad and will suffer deservedly for their sins. If you are suffering, it is because you are guilty and should suffer."[2]

As a young psychotherapist, I trained with Carl Whitaker, one of the grandfathers of the family therapy movement. He said we can't fully understand ourselves unless we look at the legacy left to us by past generations. When he worked with a family, he would ask three generations of family members to attend the sessions. He believed that any unfinished emotional business lived in the collective unconscious of the family, passed on to the next generation. In my case, that was a boatload of alcoholic shame. It came into my bones by emotional osmosis.

We Feel Shame If We Have Been Treated Badly by Others

Examples of bad treatment are being neglected or emotionally, physically, or sexually abused.

Physical abuse evokes shame in a victim, purely from the experience of someone helping themselves to our body. For some victims who both love and hate the perpetrator, the violation also causes confusion.

If your fundamental emotional needs are ignored, the neglect evokes shame about even having those needs. To children, it feels like something must be wrong with them: *Why wouldn't Mom or Dad pay attention to me?* The person who is neglected thinks, consciously or unconsciously, *Maybe I want too much. Maybe they don't like me. Maybe I am unlovable.* Over time, shame attaches to the very sensation of our emotional needs.

Emotional mistreatment may be less concrete, but it, too, can be profoundly damaging. When we are small and defenseless, we might be told we are stupid, or silly, or bratty, or (fill in the blank). If this happens, we absorb the shame like a porous sponge soaking in water. The shame becomes internalized. We believe the story we were told about ourselves. As adults, we find that a version of the story often becomes our own.

In my family it was *not* a good idea to admit a failing or mistake. People just didn't make apologies or amends. Any tiny admission was viewed as weakness, an opportunity to blame. Grievances were remembered for years, resurrected and reiterated during arguments. We were punished harshly or berated with sharp-edged, sarcastic wit. One of my father's favorite admonishments was, "What the hell's the matter with you? What've you got in between those ears? *Sawdust!*"

I learned to be constantly on guard. Deep down, I came to believe I was forever flawed. For me, as for many children of alcoholics, shame became deeply internalized, etched into an identity of "not good enough." No redemption for my sins; no kindness for my shortcomings.

Many of us in the Twelve Step program experience this underlying sense of defectiveness, referred to in *Twelve Steps and Twelve Traditions* as "the feeling we don't quite belong." Findings from a study by the University at Buffalo's Research Institute on Addictions (RIA) support the connection between underlying feelings of shame and misusing alcohol or drugs, concluding that "individuals who are prone to shame when dealing with a variety of life problems may also have a tendency to turn toward alcohol and other drugs to cope with this feeling."[3]

When we feel shame it can be an overpowering sensation. Perhaps we feel defective, or our skin burns, or we want to drop through the floor and disappear, put a bag over our head. Shame is both an emotional and physiological state, and that is why using drugs or alcohol to block it out is so appealing. Chemical use can physiologically alter shame, make it stop hurting for a while. And how great is that—if not for the long-term effects?

We Engender Shame When We Act Badly toward Ourselves or Others

Perhaps we keep the old family ways alive with neglectful habits, not eating or sleeping properly. Abusing alcohol or drugs, with all the secrets and personal destruction it entails, is sure to engender a deep feeling of failure and shame. Self-destructive acts or explosions of angry violence make us feel bad about ourselves, even if covered by layers of defensive denial. Some of us try to compensate for our badness by going the opposite way, becoming overachieving perfectionists, "driven by shame and a desire to cover up a deep hole in our soul."[4]

In any case, we can remember a crucial distinction: appropriate guilt occurs when we feel bad about a specific *behavior,* creating motivation for change. When shameful, on the other hand, we feel bad about *ourselves* after a specific event.

Entering the Dragon's Cave—a Path beyond Shame

I scored in all three of the areas just described. These sources of shame converged, creating the causes and conditions of my addictive mind. The Buddhist notion of dependent co-arising suggests that *all phenomena* are caused by a confluence of circumstances. Nothing is independent or fixed in nature. Even our character defects have "co-arisen" as a response to a particular life condition. Maybe they covered our shame, protected our vulnerability, or just plain helped us survive.

The philosophy of dependent co-arising does not give us carte blanche to blame others for our faults or duck responsibility for our deeds. Rather, seeing our interdependence deepens compassion toward ourselves and others. If we acknowledge the many, varying forces that have shaped us— both the good and the bad—we can let go of some of our harsh judgment or righteousness. Without the light of compassion, it is difficult—if not impossible—to take a fearless and searching moral inventory.

Yet I had very little compassion for myself early in my recovery. The idea of doing Step Four, taking a hard inner look at my virtues and flaws, sounded dreadful. Admit the ugly parts of myself? Face my dragons? No way. The dragon-in-me was a monster.

In medieval times, when legends of dragons and dragon slayers abounded, dragons were described as surrounded by storm clouds, with claws of lightning and a voice that roars like a hurricane, "scattering the withered leaves of the forest."[5] And the Twelve Steps tell us to stare this smelly, dirty, scaly beast in the eye? March right up and hug my shadow? What do you think I've been running from?

Even so, the toxic nature of shame, especially when it has been deeply internalized, makes facing it even more necessary. The Twelve Step program's founders say that unless we make a searching and fearless personal inventory, "there can be little sobriety or contentment for us."[6] We have to stop running, do an about-face, and step into the green dragon's cave— become intimate with our shame-based shadow self. No more blaming others for our fate. No more tap dancing. In Step Four we confront, "some of us for the first time, the darker truths about ourselves—the resentments and envies, wrongdoings and fears that have torn us apart."[7] By entering the dragon's cave, we start to become free.

The more we run screaming from this intimate encounter with ourselves, the stronger the shadow becomes. It leaks through into our relationships, drives our impulses, and feeds our addictions. Our shadow is in charge when we lose control of our temper, obliterate ourselves with drugs or alcohol, or compromise too much in a codependent relationship. The dragon rears its ugly head when we are mean to ourselves over a small mistake or speak harshly to others.

In Eastern psychology, these kinds of behaviors are rooted in a lack of awareness, or "confusion."[8] Buddhists believe that if we face our confusion, an awakened life is possible. If not, we are choosing an "ordinary life," one swaddled in delusion.[9] For many of us, this ordinary life was one of addiction or raging codependency and unconscious enactment of toxic patterns, re-creating the conditions of our childhood. Maybe we are still trying to get an unavailable person to love us. If we lived in a violent home, perhaps we unconsciously partnered up with an abusive spouse. We carry on neglectful treatment of ourselves and burn the candle at both ends, putting ourselves last when it comes to self-care.

All this can seem familiar—normal. Not realizing there is another way to be, we live with our automatic pilot set on "doomed to repeat." Buddha said it this way: "Because they are not mindful, [people] say and do things that create their own suffering."[10]

Facing Our Ambivalence about Step Four

In Step Four we are asked to look at parts of ourselves we are uncomfortable with, the parts that we reject and keep hidden out of fear or shame. Despite the high stakes, however, many of us feel highly ambivalent about facing our dragons and *really* doing a fearless and searching moral inventory of ourselves. This was touched on during a dialogue about Step Four at one of our Twelve Steps and Mindfulness meetings:

> *Matt:* One of the things I noticed by doing a Fourth Step is
> that I have a tough time finding a balance. I swing from
> being too passive to acting too aggressive. Sometimes I am
> both—passive-aggressive. The way I grew up, we never had
> any good discussions about conflict. I learned to just let

everything be dead in the water. Ten minutes later, I think, *Ah, I should have said this. Oh, I really should have defended myself this way or that way.* It's tough to like myself; I feel inadequate. I'm uncomfortable saying that. It's not something I should be afraid to say out loud, but it's very uncomfortable.

Thérèse: Because you're scared?

Matt: Yeah, because I'm scared.

Thérèse: Seeing your fear is a form of going into the dragon's cave, acknowledging your shadow. Now that you are aware of your sense of inadequacy, you can give that part of you love and kindness. To me, that is what admitting the exact nature of our wrongs begins to look like—it is an intimate self-knowing.

Matt: Yeah, because before I can even say it to someone else, as in a Fifth Step, I have to recognize it myself.

Thérèse: Exactly.

Matt: But it hurts to wake up!

Thérèse: Yes, sometimes it does.

⊕ ⊕ ⊕

Modern psychotherapy recognizes the difficulty of facing our shadow self. Psychologist Carl Jung says it this way: "The shadow is a moral problem that challenges the whole ego-personality, for no one can become conscious of the shadow without considerable moral effort. To become conscious of it involves recognizing the dark aspect of the personality as present and real. This act is the essential condition for self-knowledge, and it therefore, as a rule, meets with considerable resistance. We want to say, 'That is not me.'"[11]

Even if we are fascinated by dragons we may not want to cozy up to one, feeling the heat of its fiery breath. Here is a tale of one Chinese man actually meeting up with the dragon:

There was a man in ancient China who was fascinated by dragons. He collected paintings and sculptures of them, read and wrote poems about them, thought about them constantly.

Some dragons heard about this and one of them said, "He pays us such honor, but he's never met one of us in person. It would be courteous to visit him, I think."

So off the dragon flew and knocked at the man's door. The lover of dragons opened the door, took one look, and ran off screaming.

✤ ✤ ✤

Recently, I was working with a woman about one month into recovery. She had been putting off an assignment from her boss for several weeks, really dragging her feet. She was supposed to prepare a summary of a just-completed project that had been successful, including a brief recap of her history of working on similar tasks. He needed it to help him assess her skills for other upcoming, plum projects.

"I really have to get the report done," she said. "It only has to be a couple paragraphs, and my boss wanted it by last week. He will be making new work assignments any day now. I'm going to shoot myself in the foot unless I stop procrastinating."

I asked, "What happens when you think about working on the report? What do you experience in your body?"

She said she felt anxious, had a tight stomach. When she started to think about her work, she bumped into memories of a project that had gone badly. Quite badly, in fact. Her supervisor lied to her, a co-worker stabbed her in the back, and the budget got slashed midway. It was painful to think about, and stirred anger. So she avoided working on the report, preferring to do other things.

When I asked her to tell me more about the angry feelings, she said, "I would rather not talk about it. I want to let bygones be bygones, let it be over and done. It's in the past. What good does it do to dredge it all up again?"

"Actually, the experience with your old supervisor and co-worker feels like it's here with you right now," I responded. "It doesn't feel like it's in the far past. You may think you've let bygones be bygones, but it looks like you are sabotaging yourself instead of getting your anger out. You have to face the emotions you have about that old experience in order to get through it and learn to live without using."

She didn't want to deal with her feelings. She ran away from them again, staying loyal to her self-defeating family ways. A few months later, she quit therapy and started drinking again. She ran from the dragons who showed up at her door.

We have the choice to live an awakened life, what Buddhists call the life of a *bodhisattva*.[12] This is a choice to be mindful, see our patterns, and recognize the delusions that lead us to act the way we do. In Twelve Step terms, it is the practice of taking inventory, searching out what's driving our actions and reactions, and taking responsibility for it. Tenshin-roshi Reb Anderson says, "If we don't understand [our pain], then our energy fuels deluded activity. Bodhisattvas vow to face, to meet, to embrace, and to dance with the great green dragon of pain, anger, frustration, [and shame]."[13]

Here we begin to see that the dragon is not outside us but rather made up of disinherited parts of ourselves. We project these parts onto the faces of others, thinking our suffering is caused by our parents, our partner, or our enemies. In a fearless and searching Step Four, we begin to see and take responsibility for this truth.

Entering the dragon's cave is the way to awakening. Doing so follows the footsteps of wise spiritual sages and generations of recovering people who say that the only way to deal with the shadow side is to stop running and meet it face-to-face, seeing the truth of our inner contradictions and flaws. Mindfulness chisels through the wall of our delusions, allowing us to "tumble into the presence of light."[14] If we bring all parts of our self, including the ugly, disowned aspects—perhaps especially those aspects—into the light of mindfulness, we move out of shame into a more compassionate self-acceptance.

As we continue in meditation, "we eventually, little by little, gain more access to the deeper places of our being. We need not charge ahead, lance in hand, into the lair of the dragon. The dragon will come to us."[15] We can rest in our practice, stay with what arises, and not run away screaming.

The Eightfold Path as a Moral Inventory

In the final insight from Buddha's teaching on the Four Pure Insights into the Way Things Are, he says there *is* a path out of suffering, a way to gain liberation from our fears.[16] It is called the Eightfold Path. This path heightens our self-knowledge in eight key areas. Each area is seen as a gateway to deeper peace, providing a way to take stock of how we live.

This Eightfold Path is not, in the traditional Judeo-Christian sense, a set of commandments instructing us in right or wrong. In the Eightfold Path, "right" is synonymous with "wise." Something is "right" when it facilitates awakening, "wise" when based in clear seeing rather than delusion. Each gateway of the path is a practice in mindfulness, a process of gaining insight about what makes us suffer and what makes us happy. Failures are seen as opportunities to learn, occasions to practice kindness toward ourselves and start anew. In the Buddhist view, there is no such thing as a stain on our milk bottle.

In teaching the Eightfold Path, Buddha instructed us to take regular inventory about "how, when, and why" we are skillful and "how, when, and why" we are not. Following is an overview of each gate in the path.

Our Views

We can begin by observing our attitudes, noting which ones are rigid and closed, causing us to judge others. A mind that is free from dogmatism, intolerance, or arrogance is considered "right," or "wise." An open, flexible mind isn't hindered by preconceptions. It allows us to see the reality of each moment as it is, not as we imagine it could or should be.

Our Thoughts

Here we tune in to the many thoughts going on in our mind. We notice our mental patterns—the "stories" we tell ourselves about why things are happening—and become aware of which thoughts generate fear, shame, or anger. Once aware of our destructive thoughts, we can guard against them. Thoughts, intentions, and aspirations that are kind and free from delusion are considered to be "wise thought."

Our Speech

In this area of the Eightfold Path, we pay attention to how we talk to ourselves and others. We note the words we use in our conversations. How blaming or shaming are we of others? Are we listening or simply waiting to make our case? Speech that is truthful, nonviolent, and compassionate is considered "wise speech."

Our Actions

How often are we set on automatic pilot, not aware of our actions, especially of their impact on others? How often are we reacting without thinking? How often do we wonder later, *Why did I do that?* By contrast, which of our actions are in keeping with our values? How do we feel when we are acting with integrity? Which way do we want to be in the world? These are some of the questions we ask as we contemplate our actions.

"Wise action" happens when we are conscious of our choices, aware that our actions affect others because we are all interconnected. Buddha said there are three times we should be aware of our actions: before, during, and after we act. In "right action" we seek this comprehensive level of awareness.

Our Livelihood

Walking the Eightfold Path also means looking at the work we do in the world. We ask whether our work produces entanglements or exploits others. Is our work driven by greed? Does our livelihood foster cooperation and harmony? When we experience conflicts based on our work or the ethics of our employer, we find it hard to be at peace in our life. Buddha advised that our work, or at least the way we do our work, be for the betterment of the world. This approach is considered "wise livelihood."

Our Efforts

Here we look at which of our efforts involve pushing, forcing, or straining—trying to control the uncontrollable. "Wise effort" is free of insisting on a particular outcome. It is the Serenity Prayer in practice.

Our Mindfulness

This area of the Eightfold Path weaves together all the previous aspects. We examine how mindful we are of our body, emotions, thoughts, and beliefs. Are we here, in our life? Or is our attention placed elsewhere—in fantasies, escapism, or preoccupations with the past or the future? What effort are we making to become present? Do we make time for a mindfulness practice to help us? "Wise mindfulness" occurs when we are focused on each moment and each day instead of being worried, distracted, or intoxicated.

Our Meditation

The last area of the Eightfold Path suggests we practice mindfulness and meditation on a regular basis. "Wise meditation" is when we let go of "trying to get, trying to change, trying to control, trying to bring about" this or that.[17] We touch profound quietude when we just sit in meditation, doing nothing. We become aware of the space between our thoughts, where our true nature can be touched.

Sitting on the cushion in meditation, in itself, is a form of taking inventory. We allocate time to listen to the sensations of our body, observe thoughts passing through our mind, and see the range of emotions that comprise our human experience. We start to note patterns of body, speech, and mind. Maybe we notice, *Wow! Nearly every time I sit, I'm agitated and angry.* Or, *I'm often thinking about the people that have slighted me, nursing resentments.* Or, *Craving arises, feelings of not being good enough and wanting another person to fill me up.* Regular meditation allows us to see both our inner selves and the outer world more clearly. Unveiled. Bare.

Mindfulness Practice for Step Four: Inventory of the Eight Gates

When doing Step Four for the first time, I used the *Blueprint for Progress* published by the Al-Anon Family Group Headquarters. I don't know how I could have done a solid moral inventory without it. The *Blueprint* booklet offered a concrete structure, a set of reflective questions, and even spaces to write in on each page. Both the *Blueprint* and the help of my sponsor were invaluable.

Still, I brought my Judeo-Catholic self with me into the process, and my first Fourth Step evoked fear and shame. Particularly difficult was taking stock of each of the seven cardinal sins—pride, anger, envy, lust, gluttony, greed, and sloth—which were included in the *Blueprint* inventory at the time.

I have since found comfort in the Eastern view of "bare attention," the process of noticing whatever arises with interest and curiosity, without judgment or condemnation. This attitude is the essence of mindfulness. Over the many hours and over the many years of sitting on the meditation cushion, practicing this art of noting without judgment, I have come to a much better sense of what the founders of the Twelve Step program meant by taking a "searching and fearless moral inventory." I believe they were describing the attitude of bare attention—simply observing and taking inventory of what we have done and the suffering it caused. This is *not* the attitude of shame about our sins and counting up all the marks on our milk bottle in one grand, horrendous tally.

Buddha advises us to notice how we are doing in each of the areas of the Eightfold Path, taking inventory on a regular basis. He instructed us to observe without undo criticism and with an interest in learning. With this approach, we can make fearlessness and honesty a way of life.

I offer the following mindfulness practice as a way of taking inventory with bare attention. It is based on looking at your skillfulness or lack of skillfulness in the areas of the Eightfold Path. Consider writing down your responses to each group of questions.

Wise Views

Which of your ideas about yourself or others are particularly rigid? Can you find any examples of dogmatism, fundamentalism, bigotry, close-mindedness, or excessive criticism?

Which views of other people or other situations cause you or others suffering or harm? How? What actions are driven by these views?

What is the specific impact of rigid views on your relationships? Give examples of views that caused a negative impact.

What views of yourself cause you suffering or harm? List them. What actions follow from these views? How do these views contribute to your addiction or compulsion? Give examples.

Wise Thought

What are some examples of thoughts that habitually run through your mind—those that rerun time and again as "different circumstances, same story." List them.

What influences formed these habitual thoughts? For those that you identify as unskillful, which were spawned by

- your family's legacy?
- how you were treated by others?
- your own behaviors?

What actions are fed by the thought patterns you identified? For example, do you spend time engrossed in pursuing pleasure or avoiding pain or discomfort of any kind (such as fear or anxiety)? Which thoughts or beliefs drive these pursuits? What are the results?

Do you spend energy trying to bury your fears or other uncomfortable emotions? What thoughts or beliefs drive this energy? What are the results?

Wise Speech

Reflect on how speech was used in your family. How did people speak to each other

- during conflict?
- when in need?
- if happy or unhappy?
- when holding others accountable?

What habits or patterns of speech do you notice in yourself in each of the above areas?

What happened to your speech during your addiction or codependency? Were you untruthful either by commission (something you said) or omission (something you failed to admit)? Give examples.

How can you incorporate mindfulness into how you speak to yourself and others in your daily life? For example, you could practice "right speech" by using nonviolent communication.[18]

Wise Actions

Think of areas of your life, one situation at a time, where you may be astray from your buddha nature and where right action may be necessary. What actions are weighing you down in each situation? Possible examples are denying reality, telling falsehoods, living in excess, taking what is not given to you, speaking ill of others, and repressing your feelings or ideas.

What will help you take the right action in each situation? Could you be more skillful at

- telling the truth?
- giving to others?
- being compassionate toward others' suffering or your own?
- living simply?
- accepting what you cannot change?
- letting go of a relationship that is violent, destructive, or codependent?
- being sober?

In each situation you described, what specific behaviors help you take right action?

Notice the effect of some of your daily actions: What actions help you live your values? What actions hurt you or others?

How can awareness help you identify when you are not in accordance with your true self? Do you feel physical sensations such as a tightness in your stomach when you behave in ways that are not skillful? If so, describe those sensations.[19]

Wise Livelihood

Notice what you think about money and how you spend your financial resources.

How was money viewed in your family of origin? Did family experiences leave you with beliefs such as "Money is the root of all evil," or "I can only be happy if I have a lot of money"?

How much of your money do you spend on the things that you *say* are important to you? How much of your money is going toward things that you don't really value? How do you feel about the reality of where your money is going versus where you would like it to be going?

How much of your money is given to causes you believe in, those less fortunate, or to helping others in recovery? How do you feel about what portion of your money is given away?

Also take inventory of the way you spend another key resource—your time. Look at your calendar or appointment book. How much of your time do you spend on the things that you *say* are important to you? How much of your time is going toward things that you don't really value? How do you feel about the reality of where your time is going versus where you would like it to be going?

Do you have a right balance between the time that you give to yourself and what you give to others? Why or why not?

In summary, which of the investments of your time and money are "wise livelihood"? Which are questionable? For example, which uses of your time or money

- create entanglements, obligations, or messy transactions?
- are rooted in exploitation of others?
- have been spent on pursuit of your alcohol or drug habit?
- have been spent on winning over or pleasing someone else?
- feed endless desires for "more, more, more"?
- cause suffering versus cooperation and harmony?

Wise Efforts

The gateway of "right," or "wise," effort is closely tied with wise mindfulness. What efforts have you made to

- achieve full awareness of arising feelings?
- face obstacles in your life rather than use addiction, compulsive activities, or relationships to "fix" a difficulty?
- foster healthy states of mind, such as gratitude and humility?
- commit yourself to positive action?
- let go of dualistic, either-or thinking?

Which of the above efforts have been "wise," cultivating awakening versus numbing out? Which have not? Why?

Wise Mindfulness

How strong is your capacity to detach and observe what is happening *inside* you (your body sensations, thoughts, and emotions)?

How strong is your capacity to detach and observe what is happening *around* you?

Which of your activities support and develop mindfulness? Which of your activities hinder mindfulness?

Give some examples of when you have reacted mindlessly. Also describe times when you have been mindful. Which choices created a better quality of life? Why?

How developed is your ability to hold an attitude of "bare attention" toward what arises, in yourself and in your life? Remember that bare attention is the ability to notice what is happening in the moment, without judgment or stories of interpretation, simply noting:

- What is your reaction in this moment to what is going on?
- Does it make you sad, glad, mad, guilty, ashamed, or afraid?
- What story are you telling yourself about the event or your reaction?
- Where or how did you learn this "story"?

Wise Meditation

What spiritual practices nourish you? For example, are you

- taking part in a faith community?
- spending time in nature?
- meditating?
- taking quiet time each day?
- doing yoga?
- following your bliss?
- chanting or singing hymns?
- doing service work?

Describe any of your spiritual practices that are not found in this list.

What inspiration do you draw from spiritual practices?

Are you satisfied with the effort you invest in your spiritual practice, formal or informal?

What additional action do you want to take to strengthen your spiritual practices?

5

Placing Ourselves
in the Cradle of Kindness

Step Five	We admitted to God, to ourselves, and to another human being the exact nature of our wrongs.

KINDNESS CAN HEAL MANY ILLS. There weren't any other seven-year-olds in line, waiting with a knotted-up stomach. The vestibule of Saint Richard's church was cool and soothing, even during humid, sticky summer days. High ceilings, arched with massive wooden beams, let the space breathe. The interior was hushed, perfumed by scents of incense and candle wax. The confessionals were on the left side, next to the bigger-than-life statue of a serene Mother Mary draped in sky-blue satin dotted with gold stars, holding baby Jesus in her arms.

Once the priest arrived, I entered the closet-size confessional room, closed the dark velvet curtain, and knelt on the padded bench. Father Bender slid the small window open, leaning his ear close to hear my murmurs. I made the sign of the cross over my forehead and chest.

"Forgive me, Father, for I have sinned. It has been two days since my last confession."

He leaned closer. I thought I noticed a slight frown cross his face. But it was dark and hard to see.

"Yes, my child."

"I have lied to my parents twice. And I had immodest thoughts of naked ladies in my dreams last night."

"Have you had these thoughts often?"

"No, Father. Last night was the first time."

"Is there anything else?"

"No, Father."

"All right. Say an Act of Contrition and two Hail Marys for your penance."

"Yes, Father."

In that instant, I heard the unthinkable. Father Bender, a kind man in his late fifties—he seemed ancient to me—started *chuckling*. Shoulders jiggling, a soft whisper of a laugh.

"And dear . . . don't come back for a while."

EVEN AT THAT INNOCENT "AGE OF REASON," I showed signs of the overly scrupulous conscience that was to come. Already, I felt the shame of being in an alcoholic family. I wanted to do something to make the arguing and drinking stop. I wondered, If only I could get it right (whatever that is!), maybe my dad will stop drinking. I felt somehow that the chaos at home was my fault . . . maybe I could make it better by being "more good." The seeds of mythical power were sown, rooting an exaggerated sense of responsibility and its converse—free-floating feelings of failure.

Father Bender's words were a counterpoint, relief for a passing moment. I revealed my sins and he was gentle. I remember, still, the sweet sound of his chuckle.

In Step Five, we are asked to bare our soul to God, ourselves, and another human being. Reveal all, put it out there, and take the risk to show our shadow self. No covering up.

In *Twelve Steps and Twelve Traditions,* it says, "Few muddled attitudes have caused us more trouble than holding back on Step Five. Some people are unable to stay sober at all; others will relapse periodically until they really clean house." Old-timers, sober for years, "will tell how they tried to carry the load alone; how much they suffered irritability, anxiety, remorse, and depression; and how, unconsciously seeking relief, they would sometimes accuse even their best friends of the very character defects they themselves were trying to conceal. They always discovered that relief never came by confessing the sins of other people. Everybody had to confess his own."[1]

The practice of confessing, admitting the exact nature of our wrongs to another person, is ancient. The founders of the Twelve Step program acknowledged the value of making a clean breast of our wrongs: "It has been validated in every century, and it characterizes the lives of all spiritually centered and truly religious people. But today religion is by no means the sole advocate of this saving principle. Psychiatrists and psychologists point out the deep need every human being has for practical insight and knowledge of his own personality flaws and for a discussion of them with an understanding and trustworthy person."[2]

A Release from the Burden of Self

I took my first Fifth Step during my second year of sobriety. It was with Marty Heist, an older, kindly man who was a practicing Quaker. I remember him as a tall person, but thirty-some years later, I'm not sure if that is actually true or merely a reflection of my emotional regard for him. Marty sported a full head of faded brown hair, peppered with gray and cut in a bowl-shape, evoking images of the Pilgrims at Plymouth Rock. He wore square-shaped, heavy-rimmed black glasses with thick lenses that magnified his eyes. I met him during a Johnson Institute workshop on the disease theory of alcoholism and resonated immediately to his understated, gentle way of being. After many years in the Twelve Step program, a fact he was quite public about during his workshop presentations, he seemed wise and insightful.

I thought carefully about how to do a Fifth Step, discussing possible candidates with my sponsor before proceeding. In hindsight, I'm grateful I took time to consider who would be a good fit for my personality and sensitivities. I needed a confessor who was nonjudging, kind, and compassionate. For me, it would have been a disaster to do a Fifth Step with a "hard-liner," adamant to impress the truth of my wrongs upon me. I had a belly full of that already.

Marty Heist was a beautiful soul. He listened with complete attention, nodded as I owned my defects and failings, and laughed with the understanding of someone who'd "been there." He, too, had walked through the valley of deep darkness, now worn but wiser because of it. Frankly, his compassion was uncomfortable and difficult to receive. I squirmed in my chair, wondered what time it was, and thought, *When is this going to be over?* He had so much more life under his belt. Maybe he could have laughed a lot more at the silliness of some of my youthful shortcomings. But he didn't.

Insight can come in many forms, and Fifth Steps come in a variety of experiences. But the spirit of the Step is to be relieved of the "burden of self." If we don't follow our Fourth Step inventory with a good Fifth Step, we risk staying stuck in shame and delusion. For me, the kindness I experienced from Marty Heist was one of my first tastes of emotional safety. At the time, my heart was like sunbaked soil, too dry and hardened to absorb the fresh water of rain. His caring washed over and ran off. The experience, even still, was a beginning, a subtle shift in how to be in the world. Instead of armored and afraid, trying to conceal my deficiencies, I began to open. A little. And then a bit more.

People tell other stories of their Step Five experience and its impact. One member of our Twelve Steps and Mindfulness Group, active in Narcotics Anonymous (NA) and Emotions Anonymous (EA), reports having an "aha" during his Fifth Step. When he was a heroin user, his circle of also-addicted friends egged him on to do outrageous things. The more provocative, the more machismo points he scored with his peers. Ben tells of going through his list of shortcomings and not feeling much remorse— a bit of pride if anything. He was doing his Fifth Step with his newfound sponsor, another hard-core addict in recovery. Ben saw the look of horror on his sponsor's face when he described his drug-induced antics. Someone who had also used heroin, lived on the streets, and seen the underside of life was aghast at his stories. Ben says it stopped him cold, shattering his denial. He realized the impact of his behaviors on others and felt "sobered" for one of the first times in his life.

Jack, another member of our Monday night group and an active member of Al-Anon, says the person who heard his Fifth Step started yawning midway through. He was bored! Jack says he was shocked. Here he thought his shortcomings and wrongdoings were of such import, and this guy was yawning. At that moment, Jack realized his shortcomings were ordinary rather than *extra*ordinary. He suffered from a classic codependent delusion, thinking his mistakes were too big and bad, even believing he shouldn't have shortcomings at all. Jack saw that he was part of humanity, no better or worse than other people. This realization was a huge relief.

Step Five as Loving Kindness

Doing Step Five is an act of placing "our fearful mind in the cradle of loving-kindness."[3] In Buddhist literature, an experience of loving kindness such as a Fifth Step is described as "touching the mind of buddha." The qualities of loving kindness (in Pali, *metta*), along with compassion *(karuna)*, appreciative joy (sometimes translated as gratitude, or *mudita*), and equanimity (translated as serenity, or *upekkha*), are called the "Four Limitless Qualities," or *brahmaviharas.*[4] They are called "limitless" because, once seeded, they grow in immeasurable ways, making our mind like the mind of the loving *brahmā* gods.[5]

DaeJa Napier, founder and guiding teacher of the Brahma-Vihara Foundation in Amherst, Massachusetts, says that experiencing loving kindness is essential to an inner transformation, like the change we seek in recovery: "Only the sweet resilient strength of [loving kindness] is capable of healing into the depths of agitation, anger, ill will, and fear that come with our human life."[6] When we admit our wrongs and receive the acceptance and kind understanding of another human being in the Fifth Step, we begin this "healing into the depths" of our addictive mind.

Taking Step Five can be the start of cultivating loving compassion toward ourselves. We discover that our very vulnerability, that uncomfortable sensation of being exposed, is actually a bridge to deeper connections with others. The Twelve Step program founders say doing a Fifth Step is "the beginning of true kinship with [people] and God."[7] Now, these thirty-some years after my first Fifth Step, emotional safety is the norm among my circle of dearest friends.

WHEN I TALK WITH MY SPIRITUAL ADVISER, senior dharma teacher Eijun Linda Ruth Cutts from the San Francisco Zen Center, I make it a point to bring up the things I don't want to say. One spring morning, we visited in her home at Green Gulch Farm in northern California, just a few weeks after my mother died.

The black arrow on the white wooden sign pointed right, and block letters spelled out "Private Residences." Gravel crunched under my shoes along the path leading up the long incline to the bamboo gate.

The gate creaked as it swung open; a canopy of flowering vines entwined overhead, offering an embrace of welcome. Gray slate stones marked the path to Eijun Linda Ruth's bungalow. Oriental poppies, tall as my shoulders, graced the door; rich plum petals reached toward the sun.

At the door, we bowed in greeting. I removed my shoes, sliding on pink-striped Japanese sandals for walking indoors. Linda Ruth offered hot peppermint tea and fresh-picked blueberries on an itty-bitty saucer painted yellow and blue. I had no idea we would talk for nearly two hours.

But her still presence and deep listening caused all the old feelings and hidden shames to come tumbling out. How I was sad that I no longer had a momma, the loving, gentle woman who died at ninety-one. She was too gentle, couldn't stand up to my father's cruelty when drinking. I confessed that I had to *make* myself visit the nursing home in her final years. That witnessing her decline was heartbreaking. That although I loved my mother, I was relieved at her passing.

I went on, telling Linda Ruth what it had been like to realize, at the age of eight, that my father had a drinking problem. When he didn't show for my Confirmation service at Saint Richard's church, it dawned on me that other dads didn't act like that. I waited in the school hallway, clad in a white choir gown, crimson collar, and matching beanie, keeping a watch out for him, scared and wondering, *What happened? Did he get in an accident? Forget all about me?*

My friend's dad, Mr. Cretzmeyer, lanky, bald, with a lopsided grin, took pity on me. I could see the you-poor-little-bird look in his eyes. He took a snapshot of me with his Polaroid camera: standing alone, hands folded in posed prayer, wide-eyed with fear. After the ceremony, just as my class filed out of the church, my father arrived. He was staggering and slurring his speech, reeking of booze. I wanted to drop through the floor. Embarrassed to death. Resentful. My mother wasn't at the church; she was at home doing last-minute preparations for the after-party with the relatives. When my father and I walked in, I was sure she could see that he was drunk. But she acted like nothing had happened; everything was ducky.

I told Linda Ruth how I didn't dare invite other kids to my house after that. I went to my friends' homes instead, any chance I could get. One set of parents said they didn't want me around because I came from a bad family. But my pal Jody fought back, defying her parents. Finally, they relented. I attached to my friends' parents, wishing they would adopt me. As I grew older, I held up a well-crafted false self: smiley face, polite manners, good grades. I hid the desperate, seething, scared child within and became a pretender.

I confessed feelings of disgust, mixed with a sense of superiority, toward my sister Cecile and younger brother Joey when they didn't help my mother during her last years. And she was a lovely lady. She was a great enabler of my father's alcoholism, yes, but also a gracious woman. My sister and brother visited her in assisted living only once or twice and didn't help with the various moves or cleaning out the family house of fifty years. They didn't come to her deathbed to say good-bye. Neither of them came to her funeral. Their absence broke a social taboo—even if people hate their mother, they come to her funeral. But not my sister or brother.

And now I was completely stymied by the seeming impossibility of having even a civil relationship with either of them. To Linda Ruth I described how I bounce between blaming myself (*What else could I have done?*) and blaming them (*What the hell is wrong with them?*). That if my other sister Anne and I didn't join in dissing them, I wasn't sure we'd have much left to talk about. What if there was nothing else to hold us together?

Eijun Linda Ruth, holding a steady gaze with her clear hazel-green eyes, sat with legs crossed in lotus style on the chair. Dressed in olive-brown *samue,* a loose-fitting Japanese work garment, she had not an ounce of judgment in her presence. She held pure compassion and understanding, sometimes joining with a story of her own—times that she, too, felt exhausted from grief, struggled with anger, or slipped into less than skillful speech. She embodied an utter lack of pretense and the wisdom of an honest heart. I felt completely safe, willing to reveal the exact nature of my wrongs.

Two hours later, I closed the creaky gate on the way out. As sun rays streamed, warming my face, I was surprised at how much and easily I had talked. I remembered how, in the past, I used amphetamines to loosen up, to be able to join in conversation at parties. By contrast, it had been easy to speak freely with Linda Ruth. The loving quality of her presence inspired openness, giving space for my heart to blossom.

The stains on the milk bottle dissolved. Like magic ink that disappears when you hold it in the sun.

Growing Loving Kindness through Meditation

Perhaps the experience of loving kindness in Step Five is one of the first in our conscious experience. In order for the grace of kindness to penetrate our addictive shame, we need to cultivate this first of the Limitless Qualities. We can foster loving kindness in our life by developing loving relationships with others—members of the Twelve Step program, our sponsor, our spiritual teachers, and our friends and family. And we can grow loving kindness directly through meditation.

Loving kindness meditation brings many benefits to our brain and our being. Many of the recent, astounding findings from brain research are drawn from studies of Tibetan monks engaged in loving kindness meditation. These experienced meditators—monks who were trained in loving kindness meditations since they were teeny tots—have a high level of neural activity in their left prefrontal lobe, the "happy place" of the brain. They also have an elevated baseline of gamma wave activity. A high gamma wave is experienced as an "aha" state of clarity and insight.

In loving kindness meditation, we move away from pure mindfulness practice. Mindfulness fosters being present and aware of the moment without judging it as good or bad; we just notice. Though awareness is the foundation of all meditation, loving kindness is a different form of meditation called "concentration practice." Here we hold an intentional, concentrated thought in a particular direction. We *do* think about something, giving a job to our busy "monkey mind," the distraction that takes place when attention jumps randomly from one point of focus to another.[8] We train ourselves to direct kind, befriending thoughts toward ourselves, etching new neuropathways in our brain. We say a loving kindness blessing and repeat it like a mantra, over and over again. In time, loving kindness soaks into our mind, into the depths of our heart and soul.

Thích Nhất Hạnh says, "When we're silent, we are able to calm our body and our mind. But *if you are content only with this, you will not be able to go far in the work of transforming the depths of your consciousness.*"[9] When we practice mindfulness, we see how we are "wired" and perhaps become less judging about what we find. Mindfulness begins inner transformation, but if we don't go deeper, we won't be able to plumb the depths of our mental habits. For the deeper level of change, we add the practice of concentrated loving kindness. Later on, we can build on the base of loving kindness with other meditations on the Limitless Qualities of compassion, appreciative joy, and equanimity.

Loving kindness meditation is a form of guided meditation. In the early days of Buddhism, guided meditations were commonly used. Thích Nhất Hanh explains why: "In the practice of guided or concentrated thought meditation we have the opportunity to look deeply into the mind, to sow wholesome seeds there, to strengthen and cultivate those seeds so that they may become the means of transforming a suffering in us."[10] According to the stories handed down to us from ancient times, Buddha gave this practice as an antidote to fear. A group of monks went off into the forest to meditate. While there, a big storm brewed. Rain poured down, thunder boomed, and lightning cracked across the sky. The trees rattled, bending to the ground.

The monks ran back to the Buddha, saying, "We can't meditate in that forest; it's *haunted*."

"No problem," the Buddha said, "come sit down. Let me teach you something to do, a meditation that will protect you from fear."

I find the imagery of the haunted forest particularly interesting because our habits of mind are often rooted in ghosts of the past, shaped by how we were raised. In a sense, we are haunted by ideas we learned as a child, now internalized as truisms.

The Ancient Structure of Call-and-Response

So how do we practice loving kindness *(metta)* meditation? To begin, remember that each line of a loving kindness meditation starts with "May I." This poetic structure uses an age-old, rhythmic pattern of call-and-response found in both Judeo-Christian and Buddhist scriptures. In biblical texts such as the Book of Ruth and Psalms of David, we hear people of old call to God. In the next verse, we hear God's answer. Call-and-response is defined as the "spontaneous verbal and non-verbal interaction between speaker and listener in which all of the statements ('calls') are punctuated by expressions ('responses') from the listener."[11]

The Buddhist belief is that there must be a response when we call out because we are part of the great web of interbeing. There cannot *not* be a response. Hindu and Buddhist mythology use the metaphor of Indra's web to depict this interdependency. In Eastern lore, Indra is the Vedic god of all creation. In his web, each of us is a jewel connected to all other jewels with threads of energy. If one part of the web is tugged, a tremor is felt in all the other parts. The whole web moves. We're calling to the energy of loving kindness in the Universe when we recite these blessings. We're saying, "Hey, remember me? Over here. Come my way!"

However, we're not calling to a being or an entity outside ourselves. Buddhism holds that when we call out, we're raising the energy inside ourselves. We're saying, "May loving kindness arise in me. May it grow itself in me." Once the seeds of loving kindness are watered in our consciousness, the quality grows exponentially, in immeasurable ways.

Mindfulness Practice for Step Five:
Loving Kindness Meditation

There are three parts to loving kindness practice. Try this:

First, contemplate the following stanza of loving kindness blessings. Repeat each line slowly and silently in your mind at least three times.

May I be free from mental torments, safe both within and without.

May I be happy and peaceful.

May my body be healthy and strong.

May I have ease of well-being in this life.

Second, work with one line that calls to you. Some people are drawn to a particular line in that stanza of four. They might work with that line, steeping it in meditation for six months or a year. If you feel resistant to one of the blessings, you may even choose that one to work with more deeply. Maybe you feel angry when you hear it. Or sadness wells up. Or it seems confusing. If that's the case, there is something happening in the resistance. It's got juice. Stay with it.

Third, direct loving kindness energy toward a particular mental, emotional, physical, or life difficulty. You can do the following:

- Send loving kindness to agitation in your mind. While silently reciting the first blessing, "May I be free from mental torments, safe both within and without," imagine loving kindness energy streaming toward your anxieties and concerns. We are asking to be relieved of our fears, the thoughts that plague us. Fears are mental torments that haunt our mind. Holding an intention to be "safe both within and without" doesn't mean we are casting some Harry Potter–like magic spell. Rather, a calm mind can better recognize where danger lies, become aware of mental obsessions that stem from past trauma, and make safer choices.

- Send loving kindness to distresses of your heart. As you repeat the second line, "May I be happy and peaceful," send loving kindness to your heart and your emotions—each of your sorrows, hurts, or resentments—asking that you be healed. In this line, we are asking for more than relief from troubling emotions. The classical translation is: "May I be happy and never be separated from the source of true happiness." We are asking to recognize what actually makes us happy, and that may be a surprise. We may find that as we do this meditation, our desires change over time. We start looking for the real thing, not the illusions of drugs, alcohol, food, sex, or relationships.

- Send loving kindness to discomfort in your body. You can stream loving kindness toward your body as you say, "May my body be healthy and strong." You can think, *May I treat this precious body with kindness,* or *May I be patient and friendly with this physical difficulty.* If you have a specific ailment or health condition, working with this blessing may be of great benefit. Or perhaps you have trouble caring for yourself physically. You might be reenacting neglectful, alcoholic family patterns such as burning the candle at both ends, forgetting to eat, or failing to exercise. Sending loving kindness energy toward the struggle may help it change.

• Direct loving kindness toward difficult circumstances in your life. If you are in a life situation that's troublesome, you can work with the last line, "May I have ease of well-being in this life." Hold this blessing in your mind. Send loving kindness to the difficult circumstance, such as a relationship with your spouse, friend, or co-worker. Maybe you don't know what kind of work you want to do or how to make a decent livelihood. Here we can call for ease of well-being in our life. We're not asking that we win the lottery or get handed a life on easy street. Rather, we are asking to be "in the flow" with our true self, living an authentic life in keeping with our deepest-held values. We usually have great "dis-ease" when we are fighting our true self.

❖ ❖ ❖

As you work with loving kindness meditation, consider that many reactions are possible. Some people experience deep joy in opening their hearts, others touch the sorrow of not having known loving kindness in their lives. Others feel not much of anything. Every experience is okay; none mean you are doing the meditation incorrectly. The Buddhist teaching is clear to say that "inclining our mind" in the direction of loving kindness is enough for it to take root. Our job is to keep watering it.

To get the feel for this practice, read the following text of a guided loving kindness meditation from a class at Mind Roads Meditation Center.

(Mindfulness bell sounds.)

When you hear the sound of the bell, settle in to that space of connection with yourself. Let the body hold the shape of a mountain: rooted, balanced, and upright. Alert and yet relaxed, sitting on the cushion or in the chair.

Notice your breath at this moment. Where in your body do you feel it? Once you find it, begin to follow it with the stream of your awareness. Notice breathing *in*. Notice breathing *out*. Slightly extend the next out-breath; follow it to the end where there is momentary pause. Then wait for the in-breath to fill you.

Place your fearful self in the cradle of loving kindness. Imagine sitting in a great field with all of the other meditators through all time sitting there with you. When you sit on your cushion, you join them. You can let the veils of space and time open, sensing the presence of all of the most loving people that you have ever met, or wish to meet. It could be people who are in your life now—your dear grandparent, a friend, your sponsor or mentor, your partner. Perhaps you see great spiritual beings such as Mother Teresa or the Dalai Lama, or figures from your spiritual tradition, such as Jesus, Mary, or the Holy Spirit. All are sitting with you, breathing *in* as you breathe *in*, breathing *out* as you breathe *out*.

Now that you have placed yourself in loving kindness, begin to direct that energy toward yourself. Silently say, "May I be free from mental torment, safe within and without." Concentrate on holding that intention toward yourself. Repeat the phrases, "May I be free from mental torment," "May this mind be free from fear," "May I be safe and protected from all harm, both within and without."

If you wish to coordinate the blessing with your breath, as you breathe *in* say, "May I be free," and as you breathe *out,* "from mental torment." Follow the breath, turn the phrase. Direct it toward the worries and preoccupations of your mind. Send loving kindness toward both real and imagined fears.

Move your concentration to your heart center, sending a wish: "May I be happy and peaceful. May this heart know joy; may it blossom. May I be happy and peaceful. May I be happy and peaceful." Breathing *in*, "May I," breathing *out*, "be happy and peaceful."

Direct loving kindness energy toward any lingering hurts, resentments, or losses. Say, "May I be healed. May *this* heart be happy and peaceful. Light. May I let in grace and joy." Hold these intentions in your mind. Imagine loving kindness streaming into your heart-center.

Next, send loving kindness to your body, saying, "May this body be healthy and strong." Repeat the blessing several times in your mind. If you are suffering from pain or a plaguing health condition, send loving kindness to it. If you have unhealthy or neglectful physical habits, send them loving kindness. Hold the concentrated thought, "May this body be healthy and strong. May I treat my body with kindness." Breathing *in,* "May I be healthy," breathing *out,* "and strong."

Shift your awareness to your life circumstances, your relationships, job, church, community, or Twelve Step activities. As you breathe *in,* say, "May I have ease of well-being," and as you breath *out,* "in *this* life, in *this* world." Turn that blessing over in your mind several more times.

Gather all these intentions and concentrate on sending loving kindness energy to yourself. Slowly recite the blessings one more time: "May I be free from mental torment, safe both within and without. May I be happy and peaceful. May my body be healthy and strong. May I have ease of well-being in *this* life."

On the next out-breath, expand the circle of loving kindness to include people still suffering from addictions. As you breathe out, send them the wish: "May you experience the energy of loving kindness. May you, too, be safe and happy and healthy and live with ease." With the next breath, send loving kindness to others in recovery, and to all beings everywhere: "May they experience the energy of loving kindness."

Take the next few moments, as we end this meditation, to go back to the breath and rest the mind. Just let your thoughts relax. Notice the breath in the body, breathing *in,* breathing *out.*

(Mindfulness bell sounds.)

6

Turning Over a New Leaf

Step Six	We were entirely ready to have God remove all these defects of character.

SOME IDEAS WE HAVE ABOUT OURSELVES are harder to let go of than others.

My husband Jim *loves* to ride his bicycle. It makes him feel free, like a kid. In his seventies now, Jim still goes on long-distance cycling trips, traveling to a host of places around the world. Seeing him follow his bliss is a wonder to behold.

Several years ago, Jim and his cycling buddies toured Portugal for the month of October. Cell phone technology being what it is, Jim could call from just about anywhere.

One morning he rang up, saying, "Hi, my love. We're having a great time. Everything is going good. No breakdowns on the bike. Body's holding up—only a few aches and pains, nothing to worry about. Weather's great, all blue skies and sunshine, and the countryside is beautiful in a desolate sort of way. I love Portugal. The people are amazing. Very friendly, even though we have to communicate with lots of gestures and pantomiming."

"Great, hon. You sound happy in your voice."

"But I had the most troubling dream last night."

"Yes?"

"I dreamed you got involved with another man while I was away. He was handsome and tall, sort of a bad-boy type."

"Oh?" I thought he was joking.

"Yeah, in the dream, you left me for him. You thought I was boring because I'm such a nice guy. You know, helpful and everything . . . too nice."

I realized he was serious.

"I was really upset by it. Couldn't get back to sleep. You wouldn't do that, would you?"

(We'd been married more than twenty-five years by then.)

"Honey, really, you have nothing to worry about."

(Pause.)

"Jim, you're not really *that* nice."

Characteristic of Jim, he started laughing. At himself. He has a beautiful, musical laugh. We still joke about that conversation. Jim says it was a moment of spontaneous clarity, a delusion dear to him illuminated.

Cutting through Confusion with Awareness

In Step Six, we realize that the image we have of ourselves is not actually as solid as it seems. The ideas we hold about who we are, or who we should or shouldn't be, are not fixed, unchangeable truisms. They just *feel* rock-solid, as if etched into our neurology. In fact, when our mind runs and reruns a certain belief, it is creating an actual neural pathway in our brain, a well-worn groove that *seems* as if it is hardwired in.

Some of our delusions have settled in and made themselves at home, all comfy and cozy with their feet up on the coffee table. They are so familiar, appearing to be "the truth," that we are not able to imagine life without them. The founders of the Twelve Step program, in *Twelve Steps and Twelve Traditions*, say, "Even . . . the best of us will discover to our dismay that there is always a sticking point, a point at which we say, 'Nope, I just can't give this one up *yet*.' And we shall often tread on even more dangerous ground when we cry, 'This one I will never give up.' . . . Perhaps we shall be obligated in some cases still to say, 'This one I cannot give up *yet*,' but we should not say to ourselves, 'This I will *never* give up.'"[1] We recognize the possibility of change in that small, simple word: *yet*.

On the path of mindfulness, we do not make efforts to "rid" ourselves of our defects, tearing them out, stomping on them and swearing *never* to act such-and-such way again. Nor do we design a rigid, perpetual self-improvement plan. Many attempts to remove our faults are but subtle acts of aggression, leading to further failure and shame. Rather, through meditation we *notice* the thoughts that generate our reactions, the feelings they evoke, and the actions that come about as a result. For the moment, we do nothing more than hold our frailty in the light of awareness.

The Eastern view is that defects of character are rooted in confusion, based on deluded ideas about ourselves and others. Mindfulness practice develops the clarity to cut through our confusion, getting to the root of it. Once we become aware of a delusion, its spell is broken. Dainin Katagiri-roshi, founder of the Minnesota Zen Meditation Center, says, "Simply through the practice of mindfulness, we begin to change. Once aware, we are not what we were."[2]

Seeing the Anatomy of a Character Defect

Meditation helps us see that *all* things are interdependent and changeable, including our shortcomings. In Buddha's Four Pure Insights into the Way Things Are, he taught that there is no separate, permanent nature in any phenomenon. For example, a defect is put in action by the thoughts or ideas we have about a particular situation. It co-arises with numerous other variables, internal thoughts and external conditions. A whole chain reaction of sights, smells, sounds, emotions, and associations with past experiences is triggered.

Daniel Goleman, in his best-selling book *Emotional Intelligence*, famously called this kind of rapid-fire reaction an "emotional hijack."[3] We are off and running, defects of character full throttle, before we even have time to think about it. An emotional hijack is triggered by the (often nonverbal) reenactment of a previously threatening experience, such as humiliation, physical violence, or verbal belittlement. In the face of one of these triggers, we want to retaliate or run away. We have a fight-or-flight response.

There is a specific chain of events in the mind and body that lead to an emotional hijack. First we experience body sensations that alert us to the fact that we are being triggered. Next a strong emotion arises. Then comes a knee-jerk instinctive or impulsive reaction.

A CLIENT OF MINE TOLD ME ABOUT VISITING HER PARENTS in Atlanta, Georgia. Leona, a fortysomething recovering alcoholic, went to spend a long weekend with her aging parents at their two-bedroom apartment in an assisted living complex. An epidemic of norovirus flu had just swept through the facility, which her parents neglected to tell her before she arrived. Her father, in his mid-eighties, had just gotten back on his feet after several days in bed with symptoms of fever, nausea, and diarrhea.

During Leona's visit, both she and her elderly mother became ill. Her father, not at full strength himself, was in the best health of the lot, and it was left to him to care for his wife and daughter.

After two days in bed, getting progressively dehydrated from the flu, Leona shuffled her way to the bathroom to use the toilet and get a drink of water. She fainted in the hallway on the way back to her room.

Her mother heard the thud and called out from her sickbed, "Leona, are you all right?"

Her father, an alcoholic who'd started drinking again after many years of sobriety, stomped down the hall. When he saw Leona crumpled in a heap, he shouted, "Get up! What are you doing on the floor? Get up! You're not really that sick. You're making a big deal out of nothing. Just *get up!*"

One of the reason's Leona's parents are in assisted living is that medical care is only a pull cord away. Yet when Leona collapsed, her father refused to contact the nursing staff that was on call at the facility. He walked away, disgusted. Leona crawled down the hallway back to her bed.

When she returned to Minneapolis two days later, she was still so ill her partner took her to urgent care immediately. The doctors admitted her to the hospital overnight, hydrating her with intravenous saline before releasing her to go home.

Once recovered, Leona uncharacteristically called her father and tried to talk with him about what happened. She said that she was angry he had yelled at her and been mean. She told him she had been in the hospital, that the doctors said she was seriously ill. She asked her father why he didn't call the nurses at the assisted living place.

People in Leona's family don't challenge her father; he rules. She knew she was out on a limb.

Her father said nothing at first, a stone wall of silence. Then he got surly, said he had tried his best, and, after all, she was fine now. He didn't think she had any cause to be angry with him. He had been sick too, and so had her mother. He thought Leona was being unreasonable.

She hung up the phone, numb inside. Within a few hours, she started spiraling into depression, feeling like an ungrateful daughter, doubting herself and her perceptions of the incident. She wanted to block out the hurt of her father's responses to her, both when she had been ill and on the phone. For the first time in many years, she thought about killing herself.

Leona's partner encouraged her to come in for an "emergency" psychotherapy session. While talking, she began to see how she turns her anger against herself in the face of her father's alcoholic denial. She recognized how neither of her parents face their emotional pain. This awareness helped her connect the dots between her childhood experiences and her past patterns of getting into emotionally and physically abusive relationships, and of staying in emotionally demanding and toxic workplaces for years on end.

Her depressive mood started to lift. Leona hadn't started drinking again, hadn't actually attempted suicide, but she wasn't free of her addictive mind. She was still trapped by her own internalized shame, denial, and self-blame.

If we are mindful, we can slow down the reactionary chain of thoughts, feelings, and subsequent actions. We can see the whole cycle as it happens, moment by moment.

In particular, meditation practice trains us to observe the "stories" that go through our mind about any given situation at any given time. We start to see the way our mind is inclined, which way it "tilts."

How our mind is inclined has been greatly influenced by our parents, for better or worse. Perhaps we have absorbed their fears and now they haunt us too. Or we expect feedback to be critical, close our ears, and defend ourselves. Maybe we learned that emotions are "too hard, too weak, too whatever" and so we want to escape into drugs, alcohol, sex, food, or a relationship. We take things personally, get shameful easily, don't allow ourselves to make mistakes.

In the throes of our automatic, hijacked reaction, we're not conscious of the stories we are telling ourselves. The thoughts are habitual. We are simply reacting how we usually do, seeing the events through the mental filter of our worldview. We don't know our thoughts are just thoughts, our take on reality, not reality. We believe ourselves. And we have to see the delusion before we can *not* believe it.

Defects as Delusions—the "Daughters of Mara"

Buddhist lore uses the male character of *Mara* to personify a deluded being. He is portrayed as layered in veils, covering and obscuring the true self and causing great harm in the world. Many philosophies or religions seek to "pierce the veil" of Mara in order to find the way to lasting peace.

Similar to Judeo-Christianity's Lucifer, the Buddhist Mara is also called a "Prince of Darkness." In contrast to the Christian view, however, Mara is not an external, all-powerful force of evil. He is seen as the "internal vices that one faces on the pathway to enlightenment. From the psychological perspective, Mara is a manifestation of one's own mind. No external demon exists since it emerges from our own deluded thoughts."[4]

Delusions are not unique to addicts, people in alcoholic relationships, or adult children of alcoholics with their own dependencies. We, as humans, are of the nature to delude ourselves. Confused beliefs underlie our defects of character, driving our addictions and other unskillful behaviors.

In Buddhist accounts, it is not just Mara who tempts us with the smoke and mirrors of delusion. He has four beautiful, clever daughters to assist him. Old tales speak of Mara sending his four daughters to lure Buddha himself off the spiritual path. Buddha resisted and became awakened. Each of the daughters of Mara represents a common, powerful human delusion, seducing us into the dream that we can control the uncontrollable.

Mara's daughter *Skandha* embodies a defended, false view of who we are. We think we *are* what we think and feel and deny our shortcomings and blame others for our troubles.

Next is *Klesha,* representing the belief that we can't "do pain"; it's too much to bear. We are enticed by our negativity, letting it overwhelm us and thinking "that's all there is."

Mara's third daughter represents the delusion that if we seek enough pleasure we won't have to feel pain. She is called *Devaputra,* a patroness of addictions and compulsions.

The delusion that we can control suffering is personified by Mara's youngest daughter, *Yama.* We are enticed into believing we can manage the change, loss, or death we fear—and these fears hold us back from living fully.

The name of each daughter is traditionally followed by *mara,* reminding us that the specific delusion has a common parent; it is part of the larger veil of ignorance that clouds our mind. Let's look into each of these shared, human delusions more deeply.

The Delusion of Skandha-Mara— a Distorted Sense of Self

The veils of skandha-mara distort our sense of self. We identify with our body, feelings, perceptions, internal beliefs, and consciousness. (In Buddhism these are called the five aggregates, or *skandhas.*) We tell ourselves the story that we can't change; it's too hard; this is just the way we are. Even if we have named our shortcomings in a Fourth Step, we may be afraid to uncover their deeper roots. We justify our actions, even in recovery, continuing to rationalize and blame others for our suffering.

At Mind Roads Meditation Center, we offer a workshop called "Dismantling Habituated Patterns." The course was created in collaboration with Byakuren Judith Ragir, now the Guiding Teacher at Clouds in Water Zen Center in Saint Paul, Minnesota. Each person in the workshop chooses a troublesome pattern or defect to work with during the twelve weeks. Participants are entirely free to select their own focus.

In a recent session, a thirtysomething married woman with two small children introduced herself by saying she was there to "dismantle her perfectionism." Her fussiness caused a great deal of stress, creating pressure to "make everything just so" and distracted her from her relationship with her husband and kids.

Over weeks of the course, however, she spent most of the time defending her perfectionism. She explained that her drive helps her get a lot done around the house, her high standards make her a crackerjack project manager, and her attention to detail contributes to her success and high income level. She was afraid, not wanting to believe her kids when they said, "Mom, let's just play. We don't want to make crafts." She didn't want to see that "doing, doing, doing" was getting in the way of her closeness with her children. She was afraid to look at this "shadow" part of herself, despite being active in Al-Anon. Her very perfectionism was driving her to say she wanted to be less of a perfectionist.

Attachment to a certain image of ourselves, the delusion of skandha-mara, leads to character defects such as defensiveness, blaming, or aggression. We are hooked into believing our perceptions of our self and others are real. We can be seduced by profound denial, maybe even thinking our problem is that we are "too nice." We were just trying to be a good person, and *bam!* everything blew up. We are a victim. We are deluded about our own part in what happens to us. We take all or none of the responsibility. We hold an inaccurate view of ourselves.

The Delusion of Klesha-Mara— Unskillful Responses to Emotions

Klesha is a Sanskrit word that means "affliction." This daughter of Mara embodies unskillful responses to emotions. We are hooked by the fear of our emotions, believing we can't handle our passions. They are too much. We tell ourselves we are not able to stand our loneliness, hurt, or anger. We think we must have the object of our craving or we plummet into despair.

Klesha-mara is like an infection: it begins slowly, but at a certain point it consumes us. Sakyong Mipham Rinpoche, Tibetan Buddhist teacher and spiritual director of Shambhala retreat centers around the world, says it like this: "When we are possessed and consumed by klesha, acting on it seems logical. Upon the basis of this faulty reasoning, we embody faulty behavior into our consciousness. Then the next time we feel aggression or desire, we have an even stronger basis for believing it's real, and the negativity arises even more quickly."[5]

In one of our Twelve Steps and Mindfulness meetings, we discussed Step Six and the shared fear people experience about feeling their emotions. Following is an exchange between myself and a member of the group, a fiftysomething woman who is a member of Co-Dependents Anonymous (CoDA):

Sonja: In many ways, I feel hijacked by my emotions. I have spent much of my life avoiding feeling, and that fed into my people pleasing. Underneath all my caretaking of others there is a lot of fear and shame. I believed for so long that I am unlovable until here, on a cushion like this, I began to see that it was a lie.

Thérèse: Yes, if we boil down our defects to their exact nature, we will likely see fear of pain, fear of our shadow, fear of death, fear of life. Step Four asks us to notice what's going on inside us so we can name and then admit to another the exact nature of our wrongs. We don't just say, "Oh, I'm such a controlling person and I do this, and this, and that." Perhaps I even understand how my personal and family history has shaped my controlling habits.

But beyond that level of awareness, we want to be mindful right in the moment when we have the urge to act in a controlling way. Right then, we want to listen deeply, asking, "What am I scared of right now? What is this fear about?" Once we have an inkling of our fear, we need to stay with it, drop the stories we have created about it, and give our afraid self loving kindness—even if our fears are irrational, as they often are.

Sonja: But what if you just can't stand it?

Thérèse: If you just can't stand to experience your fear? That would be an idea you have about your fear. If you are thinking that you can't stand your fear and the vulnerability that comes with it, you probably believe yourself. That's been a favorite delusion of mine too. With awareness and meditation practice, we learn to gently and gradually stay with our feelings a little bit longer than usual, just one or two more breaths than we think we can stand.

For example, while I'm on the meditation cushion—because in those moments I'm tuned in—I might notice the thought, I can't stand this fear, a split second before I jet off into a daydream. Let's imagine that's what happens. Next, I'm going to, gently and with kindness, pull myself back to the breath. With a lifetime of practice, hopefully, we develop the ability to stand the whole range of disruptive emotions within our self. We stop acting them out by exploding, or acting them in by self-destructing.

Instead of controlling and being afraid of life, we can meditate on impermanence. When we meditate on impermanence, we realize nothing is as solid as we think and that everything changes. Realizing the truth of impermanence is freeing. We discover that being present to impermanence feels better than trying to make everything solid and secure. Because we're not grasping or pushing away (hopefully, at least once in a while we're not!), we can enter into life, live in the present moment. We're actually here, not lost in our fantasies or addictive patterns. Actually being here is an enlightening experience.

Sonja: It's true—meditating has helped me to recognize the joy of my true nature. That's my prayer these days, "May I experience the joy of my true nature."

Group: Thanks, Sonja.

❖ ❖ ❖

If we have an ongoing meditation practice, our mind becomes more spacious. The tendency to get emotionally "hooked" with the negativity of ill will, hatred, resentments, revulsion, self-pity, or fear lessens.

The Delusion of Devaputra-Mara— Escaping into Pleasure

Wrapped in the veils of devaputra-mara, we seek pleasure from praise, food, relationships, entertainment—all forms of mood-altering substances and pastimes. Pursuing pleasure covers our fear of experiencing discomfort or dissatisfaction. We are seduced by the short-term "high," not recognizing the inevitable aftermath of increased misery. We are hooked on pleasure.

Not that there's anything intrinsically wrong with pleasure or fun. Even meditators do it! The point is to remember that the pursuit of pleasure has a dark underside.

Tibetan teacher Sakyong Mipham Rinpoche says, "We're often so devoted to the concept of pleasure that we don't notice when the pleasure is turning into pain. We keep thinking we're having a good time because we want to be, even though the pleasure is long gone. The traditional Buddhist analogy is that we're licking honey from a razor blade: it seems like pleasure, but all of a sudden it cuts us."[6]

This particular delusion runs close to home for many of us in the Twelve Step program. Devaputra fools us into thinking that drugs or alcohol will help us escape the pain of situations we cannot control. Mara's third daughter obscures the truth that suffering, or *dukkha,* is inescapable. Her veils conceal the truth that we *can* stand it with the support of the Great We, the fellowship of the program, and the power of seeing with the "Big Mind" that we cultivate through mindfulness practice.

When I worked as a chemical dependency counselor at the Family Renewal Center at Fairview Southdale Hospital in Minneapolis, Minnesota, during the late 1970s, the staff talked a lot about "shifting addictions." Examples include moving from using drugs to compulsive shopping, TV watching, eating, gambling, sex—and back again to drugs. People with shifting addictions haven't really gotten to the root of their addictive mind. Codependent people can go from one relationship to another, thinking another person will bring them happiness. Soon they are disappointed because the other person hasn't fulfilled their expectations. New relationship, same pattern. The pursuit of pleasure has moved into pain. We've been seduced by Devaputra's wiles.

It makes sense, really. The third daughter's power to "hook" is usually built upon the delusions represented by the first and second daughters. First, we believe who we think we are is real, that our sensory perceptions are the right perceptions. When we believe we're fixed and solid, it's easier to get taken in by the belief that our loneliness, hurts, and desires are permanent, unending. (That's skandha-mara.) We get overwhelmed by them, want relief. (That's klesha-mara.) Here comes pleasure, our escape, and we pursue it with fury (devaputra-mara).

Mara's daughters have moved in, taken up residence in our mind. We are hooked, fixated on what we want someone or something to be, not on what's real. Many times, we don't know what's real anymore. We're not really here in our life. We're wandering, disoriented in delusions.

The Delusion of Yama-Mara— Thinking We're in Control

Lastly, we have yama-mara, who likes to manage and control others. This daughter represents the delusion that we have power over change, loss, or death—somehow, if we could only get it right.

MY CLIENT JOHN WAS TALL, HANDSOME, AND IMPECCABLY DRESSED. The son of two adult children of alcoholic parents and the only brother of an active cocaine-using, marijuana-smoking older brother, he told me he just got fired from his job. He had been with the company a little over a year.

Six months earlier, John had gotten a sterling performance review. No complaints, nothing but praise from his superiors. He was doing an excellent job; his boss said, "Glad to have you on board. You are a big addition to our business."

But now economic times have turned tough. Profits in his industry are down and at risk. John made a mistake on some paperwork for a customer—nothing that couldn't be corrected, but the situation was egg on the face for his employer.

One week later, he was fired. No warning. No feedback with a chance to improve. This time his boss had a whole list of complaints about his performance, none of which John had ever heard before, and some of which he didn't find credible.

Unemployed for the first time in his life, John was suffering from anxiety attacks. He sat on the rust-colored sofa in my office, head in his hands.

"How could I have gotten *fired?*" he said. "What did I do wrong?"

"Nothing," I said. "You have no power over whether your boss is honest with you or not. Stuff happens that is out of your control. Much more than we wish."

WHEN YAMA-MARA ARISES, we think we are in control. We can't see the truth that everything is changing in every moment. Ultimately, we can hang on to nothing. Everything is of the nature to change. Eastern meditation teachers say that when buddhas look at the world, all they see is flux. They don't see fixed phenomena; they see continuous movement and change. Modern science supports this view, now contending that the atomic particles of our bodies, the earth, the air, are always in motion. Everything is fluid. We are powerless to stop it. Even the present moment changes in the next breath.

Yama is the Sanskrit word for death. If we are overly afraid of loss and death, then we will be afraid to live fully. Recognizing that death will happen—to us, to those who have hurt us, to those who are dear to us— may make the moments we have more poignant, more precious. But it will not prevent death from happening.

Yama-mara shows her face in fear, rigidity, judgments of self or others, and manipulative behaviors. We cling tight to our idea of how things should be. We want experiences to affirm or congratulate us, to make us feel like we've got it all under control, thank-you-very-much.

Recognizing Our Delusions

The four daughters of Mara represent the distorted stories that hook our mind. Once we are mindful of them, seeing that they are rooted in delusion, they begin to lose their power over us. Sakyong Mipham Rinpoche says, "The mind is like the wind. Unless we take hold of it, the Mara will fool us. We can avoid falling into the Mara's seductive pit-falls by using each day to meditate and then step on the path with a focus—to be mindful, to contemplate life's dreamlike quality or to look carefully at 'pleasure' before giving chase."[7]

DURING THE WORST OF A MINNESOTA WINTER, back in the day when the stock markets were strong, my husband Jim took the whole family to Troncones, Mexico, for a vacation. We stayed in a quaint, local bungalow painted yellow with blue trim. A wide veranda wrapped the front entry; several knotted hammocks hung for afternoon lazing. Not a cloud in the sky. Only the warmth of bright, happy sun, waves thrashing the shore, and tiny sand crabs skittering on the beach.

Jim's son and daughter, their respective partners, and all three grand-girls were there. Each afternoon, the young people gathered on the porch to drink beer, smoke cigarettes, and listen to rock music. IPod speakers were center stage, ringed by white plastic beach chairs, salty beach towels, and tin cans overflowing with stinky cigarette butts.

After a breakfast of rich, dark-roasted Mexican coffee, fresh papaya, and home-baked buns, we'd all traipse out to the beach. Lathering up with sun-tan lotion, we settled in to bake in the sun and frolic in the waves of the sea.

Come two or three o'clock, I'd look up from my chintzy paperback novel and see that all the kids were gone. Not a peep mentioned to Jim and me. No "Want to come up and hang with us for a while?"

I started feeling left out, miffed. I took it personally, thinking, *Well, why aren't they including me?*

Neural impulses started flooding the old neural pathways. A well-worn, default story had been triggered. It goes like this: *They must not like me very much. I've been married to their dad for more than two decades and my step-kids still don't like me. Why even bother?*

The story had a familiar ring. The left-out, not wanted, not appreciated feelings were like comfortable shoes, molded with foot imprints from so much wear. I had a lot of those feelings when I was young. Growing up in my alcoholic family felt lonely. I thought my parents didn't like me very much. They were so often preoccupied with other things, in a crabby mood, and absorbed in their troubles.

Once the dots between the feelings in the here and now connected up with the associations from my past, an old memory zipped open.

It was winter, with lots of snow and endless days of gray, overcast skies.

I was having a sleepover at my Aunt Mary's house, my dad's older sister. We had a ritual of walking down to Anderson's Drug Store on Lake Street and ordering strawberry milkshakes. We'd sit at the soda fountain counter, blow the paper wrapping off the elbow straws, and suck up a sip in tandem. At twelve years old, that was fun.

On this visit, I was sulky and withdrawn, barely said two words.

Aunt Mary asked, "What's eating you?"

I tried to tell her that my parents were always mad. Mostly Dad. My father was drinking; my mother crying in her bed. That home was chaos. I couldn't get the words to come out. It was two years before I attempted suicide, and I realize now I must have been a depressed kid.

I had already internalized my parents' behaviors as being "about me." They were preoccupied with their own difficulties and alcoholism, but I was too young to put that together. I created the only story I could to explain their lack of attention, *They must not like me very much. That's why they don't pay attention to me. I must not be very good.*

I don't remember what I said when I tried to tell Aunt Mary, but it was something like, "Nobody likes me."

She turned to me with her steel-blue eyes, pursed lips, and wrinkled brow, and said, "Oh, nobody likes you. Poooooor little ol' me. I guess I'll go eat worms."

It was a characteristically Irish response, to tease and shame, exaggerating some kind of childish rhyme she knew.

The words stung.

I wonder now, *What she was thinking? Why would she make fun of a despondent kid?* From her point of view, maybe it was something like, *How ridiculous you are, kid. We all love you.*

At the time I recoiled. Left half my milkshake untouched. I still don't like strawberry ice cream.

Now there I was in Mexico—sun shining, ocean glistening, bougainvilleas abloom. I was sitting in a beach chair, greased up with suntan lotion, sitting right next to one of my favorite people in the world, my husband, Jim. I didn't even *want* to drink beer, smoke cigarettes, or listen to rock music. I don't drink, smoke, or like rock music. I just wanted my step-kids to *want* to be with me.

I confessed to Jim: "I've been married to you all these years and your kids still don't like me very much."

Because he's lived with me for all these years, he said, "But honey, isn't that what you usually think? That it's something you've done; that people don't like you. Isn't that kind of your default?" (Indeed, it can be a pain to be married to a psychotherapist.)

Right on, Jim. At that moment, the lightbulb of awareness blinked. His comment gelled the link between the here and now and the old story of shame and abandonment etched into my bones. That's why the flickers of memory of the soda counter at Anderson Drug came into my mind, seemingly out of the blue. Awareness bobbed up to a conscious level.

I told Jim about Aunt Mary and felt the touch of his kindness. Now cognizant, I could breathe kindness to the younger aspect of me, the girl who needed tenderness from her auntie. I hadn't been silly. The hurt from home had been there for some pretty good reasons. I wasn't just a selfish, whiney kid feeling sorry for myself.

I thought, *Oh! Believing that people don't like me, that I must not be very lovable, are just ideas I have about myself. Stories I'm still telling myself from way back.* With another breath, I could send kindness to all the other stepmothers who at that moment feel they are not a part of the family, not welcomed in. To every child whose parents are overwhelmed with their own difficulties: may we all experience the grace of loving kindness.

The string of realizations popped in the course of a few minutes while I was sitting in the sand. I felt a wash of relief, like the satisfaction of pulling a nasty, stubborn weed out of a garden patch. After several deep pulls, out it comes with a jolt. All the way down to the root.

Instead of withdrawing and getting uppity with the kids, we decided to relax and invite *ourselves* over. Jim and I moseyed on up to the porch, plopped down in chairs. We had Cokes while they smoked cigarettes and drank bottles of Dos Equis. They seemed happy to see us, joked about "old folks" listening to rock music, and showed us the cool features of their iPods.

A delusion dear to me—*poof,* up in smoke. At its core, emptiness.

Asking God to Remove Defects
Starts with Mindfulness

Becoming entirely ready to ask God to remove our defects of character starts with noticing the thoughts running through our mind, observing the stories we are telling ourselves in any given moment. As we sit on the meditation cushion, we will notice thoughts arise and pass through. That's our opportunity to see the way our mind tilts, observing, *Wow, look here! I'm running that story again. It's familiar.* Perhaps it's one of those stubborn ones that feels neurologically etched into your bones. Deeply engrained, distorted stories such as those of Mara's daughters are default wiring, beliefs and internal formations that arise automatically, particularly during times of stress. They drive our actions and reactions and underlie our defects of character.

Such stories may make sense in light of our life experience. But they are stories nonetheless. We see that each one is a mental construction about ourselves, or others, or what to expect from life—a construction that seems to be solid.

Once we realize the thoughts are inherently empty, however, we can consider letting the story go. There is an opening. The veils of Mara are lifted. We become ready to abandon "our old ideas" and "let go absolutely."[8] In a moment of awareness, we're not the same as we were. Dainin Katagiri-roshi says, "Then you see, 'I can change my life!' At that time, you turn over a new leaf."[9]

Awaken to a new life.

Mindfulness Practice for Step Six:
How Does Mara Hook You?

In this meditation, we look deeply at the roots of our defects of character, piercing the delusions that feed them. Buddhism teaches that the delusions of Mara can be defeated and frustrated by awareness, seeing that all phenomena are inherently empty in nature.[10] In mindfulness training, we are encouraged to look at ourselves "objectively," to see the "many dregs of delusion stirring up muddy water: ignorance, arrogance, craving, hatred and so on."[11]

Following are questions for your reflection. I suggest writing out your answers in a meditation practice journal and seeing how they change over time.

Which of Mara's daughters is your favorite? Notice which delusion is most likely to hook you:

- Skandha-mara: You get seduced into believing your feelings, perceptions, and internal beliefs are the real you. You are deluded into thinking you are "right," act defensive, act arrogant, or deny your shadow self.

- Klesha-mara: Your emotions, especially negative feelings of anger, hurt, or craving, overwhelm you. You act them *out* (exploding, taking them out on other people) or act them *in* (imploding, taking them out against yourself).

- Devaputra-mara: You are fooled into pursuing pleasure, believing it will help you block out pain, licking the honey off the razor until it cuts.

- Yama-mara: You are taken in by an illusory sense of power that you can manage and control the suffering of change, loss, and death. If you only could get it right.

✦ ✦ ✦

Once you have identified a delusion that is dear to you, write out the details of a time when you were fooled by a daughter of Mara. If you are not yet aware of such an incident, then bring mindful attention to your reactions over the next days or weeks. See what you observe.

In either case, reflect on your experience of getting "hooked" in delusion by answering these questions:

- What hooked you? Describe what happened to trigger your reaction, such as an external circumstance or internal thought pattern.

- When you are hooked, what does it feel like in your body?
- What thoughts go through your mind?
- What feelings do your thoughts generate?
- How do you act? What do you say or do?
- What defect of character does it fuel?
- What are the consequences and effects of your reaction (to you, to others, to your relationships)?[12]

✦ ✦ ✦

Meditate on the experience of your delusion. Does it remind you of something from your childhood or earlier life experience? If so, describe that experience.

By contrast, think of a time when you were not *hooked.* Or, if you are not yet aware of such an event, be mindful over the next days or weeks and see what you notice. Then reflect on your experience of not being hooked:

- What does it feel like in your body?
- What thoughts go through your mind?
- What feelings do your thoughts generate?
- How do you act? What do you say or do?
- What about this experience is different from when you are hooked?

Reflect on the differences between times when you are hooked and times when you are not. How do the delusional ideas harm your spiritual life? Which ideas about yourself, others, or life do you wish to release? By contrast, what brings energy and serenity to your spiritual life?

7

Vowing with the Help
of All Beings

| Step Seven | We humbly asked [God] to remove our shortcomings. |

WHAT DO WE DO now that we've become intimate with our defects of character? Seen the delusions at their root? Become ready to let them go?

Buddhist teachers say, "When you see your delusion, in the very next moment, make repentance." In mindfulness-speak, this means "to be one with your buddha-nature and make your life anew."[1] This is our practice.

We are not solid, fixed beings, doomed because of how we were raised, or because we are addicts or alcoholics, or because of whatever path of harm we've walked. Impermanence is central to Buddhist philosophy, the realization that *everything* is in motion. That includes us.

Recent discoveries in Western brain science confirm this Eastern teaching of impermanence: we can rewire our emotional and behavior patterns.

In years past, neuroscientists thought the adult brain didn't change; it hit a set point and stayed that way. Modern means of measuring brain activity leads to a different conclusion. The adult brain is far more plastic than was thought. New mental, emotional, and behavioral patterns create new neuropathways. We can etch new "default" patterns in the brain itself.

This is true no matter what patterns developed when we were young, no matter what habits, compulsions, or addictions we have lived out. To that I say, "Yahoo!"

Hitting the Pause Button

One of my character defects is irritability and a quick temper. I flare up easily, especially when I am afraid, out of control, or ashamed. It's not very pretty, and it's gotten me in a lot of trouble.

When I first got straight thirty-some years ago, I was mostly passive-aggressive with my anger. Quick hit-and-runs. Because of all the arguing, yelling, and violence in my home growing up, I wanted nothing to do with anger. No sirree, not me.

I promised myself as a teen that I would never turn out like my dad. I never raised my voice, didn't speak up about what was on my mind. I swallowed my anger down, held it inside. Imploded my feelings. Consequently, I developed major somatic symptoms: stomachaches, headaches, and ulcerative colitis.

After time in recovery, I loosened up. I got better at expressing my needs and my health improved.

But the pendulum started swinging the other way. When I finally kicked cigarettes, I had more access to my angry feelings. (Surprise!) I had *a lot* of anger. It started coming out too often and too strong.

One summer, my husband, Jim, brought home a collection of stories about Suzuki-roshi, the founder of San Francisco Zen Center. It's called *Remembering the Dragon*, published on the anniversary of what would have been Suzuki's one-hundredth birthday.

One of the stories is about an interaction Shunryu Suzuki-roshi had with Ed Brown, the head cook, or *tenzo*, at the Zen Center. I've never met Ed, but people say he is quite an energetic, colorful character.

Apparently some Zen Center community members told Ed they were intimidated by his anger, afraid of him at times. He told Suzuki that he believed in saying what was on his mind, putting it out there, being forthright and direct with people.

I thought, *You bet! Me too.* There's more integrity in being direct than acting nicey-nice to someone's face and then ripping them behind their back.

Ed said *he* wasn't troubled by his anger and didn't think he had a problem. It was "just the other people" that lived with him that were bothered by it. He told Suzuki-roshi, "It seems like people are telling me that I can't have my feelings. That I can't have my angry feelings."

Suzuki-roshi replied, "Oh well, you *can* be angry. You can be angry."

(Pause)

"But maybe don't."

Me too. Now that I can have my anger, maybe I'll let it pass on through. Try holding an open heart to the underlying fear or shame instead . . . Maybe.

Whenever our particular defect starts to roar, we can say, with the help of mindfulness, "Well, I *could* say that or do that, but maybe I won't." Regular sitting meditation develops the ability to hit the "pause button" on our chain reaction. This happens not just because we are more aware but also because our brain chemistry changes with regular practice. The left prefrontal lobe in meditators is more active than in those who do not meditate. This lobe is the executive center of the brain, the control center that can override our emotional hijacks, shutting them down more quickly. We are more in control of our response. We can say, "Maybe I won't . . ."

Step Seven as Touching Our Buddha Nature

In Step Seven, we "humbly ask God to remove our shortcomings." But what are we asking? Whom are we talking to?

Buddhist philosophy does not see God as an external, omniscient, theocratic presence. There is no grandfatherly God up in the sky, all-powerful, ready to crack thunderbolts and say, "Okay, zap-a-roo, no more impatience for you, Betty."

Then what are we doing in this Step? The Eastern view of God is the "buddha nature" within us and between us. God is reliance on the spark of divinity within ourselves and in *all* living beings—people, creatures, plants, the Earth.

Buddhist philosophers use the metaphor of water to depict our shared buddha nature. Although as a human species we are made up of approximately 60 percent water, we don't look like water. When we see each other, we don't think, *Oh, look at that body of water walking around.* We don't look at a blade of grass and go, *Oh, look at that pointy bit of water sprouting from the earth.* We look at someone and think, *Jim* or *blade of grass* or *cedar tree.* We don't realize that what we're looking at is primarily water.

Just as we don't see the water that constitutes many living beings, we don't see our spiritual buddha nature. We don't think about it being there, but it is, abiding within us all. In the words of the blessed teacher Thích Nhất Hanh, the essence of our spirituality is in knowing that we are "interbeing," one with all buddhas, spiritual seekers, and ancestors of old, all abiding in the great field of wisdom and compassion. We can touch these qualities within ourselves, in others, and in the Universe.

In Buddhist practice, when we bow in a meditation hall, we are not bowing to the saint or goddess in the image on the altar. We are asking for the qualities represented by the image to arise in us. While I bow, the body and mind together express the desire that the same gentleness held in the flower, or fluidity of the water, be cultivated in me. If there is an image of compassion, such as Guan Yin, "the one who hears the cries of the world" (or Mother Mary, Buddha, Jesus, Miriam, or Krishna), it is a form of saying: "May compassion arise in me. Help me to foster something other than this impatience or anger or intolerance or perfectionism. May I be aware of the need for compassion in myself and for others, and may I water that quality in my meditation practice so that it blooms in my consciousness."

The Power of Aspiration

It seems to me that bowing is in itself one way of practicing Step Seven. Regarding this Step, the *Twelve Steps and Twelve Traditions* says, "We aspire to have our defects removed and, at the same time that we aspire toward the perfection, we have to be ready to walk in that direction."[2] No matter how haltingly.

We felt the pain of our defects in Step Six. We find it uncomfortable to be self-absorbed, or bitter, or filled with fear. We don't want to be separated from our true nature any longer; it's painful to veil it in delusion and choke its expression.

Ongoing meditation practice gives us powerful insights and fills our spirit with grace. Our motivation to practice is strengthened. We can't bear to see the suffering our shortcomings cause other people.

Now, in Step Seven, we aspire for the shortcomings to be removed, for our habituated patterns to dissolve. The Buddhist approach to this is called "aspiration practice." Like loving kindness meditation, aspiration practice is considered a concentration technique, different from the pure mindfulness of nonthinking. In aspiration practice, we are again going to give our distractible "monkey mind" a specific job to do. Instead of jumping between thoughts at random, the mind will hold, and soak, and turn the aspiration for our shortcoming to be removed. We hold this desire in a concentrated, sincere way, even if we know that in the present moment we are far, far from the change we seek.

Buddhist tradition points to aspiration practice as a way of "walking in the direction" of our desired change. We hold a strong intention to let go of the old, asking that our heart may open, blossoming into the new. We are inspired to make a vow, relying on our Higher Power to help us carry it through.

In aspiration practice, we don't just ask for something to go away. Instead, we hold an intention to open to a new virtue in its place, such as wishing to be less self-absorbed and more generous, be less riddled with fear and more trusting, have less anger in order to grow wiser, be less judging and more compassionate. If we don't have the desire yet, then we can "desire to desire" the change. Again, the old Awakened Ones say that simply inclining our mind is enough for the virtue to take hold in our consciousness.

Next, we contact the ways we have experienced the quality we desire. Pema Chödrön, an eminent teacher of loving kindness practices in the West, says, "We all have some of [the quality we aspire to], and a part of this practice is contacting it."[3] This happens when we call to mind how and when we have experienced love, compassion, or joy. By recalling the experience, we're acknowledging that we have some of the same quality within. If we did not, we wouldn't know what we were seeing. Consider an analogy: We can recognize that a flower is a rose or a daisy or a petunia because we have seen one before. In the same way, we can aspire to compassion or gratitude or kindness because we have seen these before. Touching the experience, no matter how simple, encourages our aspiration.

Once we have contacted our desired virtue, in ourselves or in response to someone else's kindness, for instance, we can expand it and cultivate its growth. Chödrön's teaching continues: "You keep going through that process of contacting whatever you already feel, encouraging it with the aspiration, noticing the effect, and then you expand it."[4]

Aspiration and Determination Create Our Vow

Our aspiration now couples with our determination. Borrowing from an ancient practice used by Buddhist monks and nuns over the centuries, we make our aspiration into a vow.[5] We make a "sacred, voluntary promise" in our own words to dedicate ourselves to our aspiration, to our sobriety and recovery.[6] And so we ask for our shortcomings to be removed.

Given the fact that we are just a person trying to do our best, however, chances are good that we are going to slip up. Our habits are long-standing patterns, ingrained both in our physiology and our behaviors. We are no longer deluded about the fierce nature of our defects of character. We tried to flee from them by using drugs and alcohol, losing ourselves in relationships, or gambling or eating them away, to no avail.

Still, we vow. This is the paradox of Buddhist practice. We know we are not where we want to be. We recognize that we will not likely succeed at getting to where we want to be. And yet we dare to aspire. We hold our promise in our heart at all times, like an unceasing prayer. We live with the tension of the gap, allowing it to expand us.

Rather than tugging or pushing with all the self-will at our command, we start by relaxing with how we are now. Breathe *in* compassion and kindness toward ourselves just as we are at this moment—riddled with shortcomings. Breathe *out* ease, letting go of unrealistic expectations. Easy does it.

A relaxed mind loosens, opening up to the *possibility* of new ideas. We can consider different ways of being in the world. We can allow the path of mindfulness and the Twelve Steps to transform us, like riding with the swift current of a stream. If we are open, we can touch the "Big Mind," the limitless potential of our own true self, and that same potential in all others. We can let ourselves be carried in the grace of a power greater than ourselves.

Pema Chödrön recommends we qualify our vow by adding, "I vow, to the best of my ability." Each time we fail at our aspiration becomes an opportunity to practice kindness toward ourselves. We begin again in each moment, much like the process of coming back to a focus on the breath in meditation—time and time again, no matter how frequently our monkey mind wanders. On the cushion, we practice calling ourselves back to the breath with a kind voice. No scolding or beating ourselves up because we lapsed into nursing our fears, stewed in our resentments, or got lost in day-dreaming.

We take the skills we developed on the cushion and bring them into our day-to-day life. When we slide into our old habits, we gently call ourselves back. Begin again in the next breath. We "give up both the hope that something is going to change and the fear that it isn't."[7] This is the way of mindfulness. This is the path to letting our mind transform, reverting back to the original default position—our buddha nature.

In Step Seven, we call to our Higher Power for comfort and support. We vow "with the help of all living beings," with the "care of the Universe," or "relying on the workings of Great Compassion" to give us aid. Here we can recall the teaching of Indra's net mentioned in chapter 5. The Eastern view of creation is that all beings are interconnected; we live in a web of interbeing. A vow tugs on one thread of the great web of interbeing with an aspiration, creating tremors in all the rest of the web. If we call, there *will* be a response.

Releasing Shortcomings through Vows

Buddhist practices suggest creating a vow in the form of a four-line verse called a *gāthā* (Sanskrit for "verse"). A deeply contemplated gāthā is considered to be an "inspired utterance."[8] I first leaned how to write and work with gāthās from Zen priest Byakuren Judith Ragir while we cotaught the "Dismantling Habituated Patterns" class at Mind Roads Meditation Center.

If you are interested in writing a vow using gāthā verse as a way to ask God to remove your shortcomings, then use the suggestions on page 104 for creating the four lines.

1. *Open*

   In the first line, describe the shortcoming or habituated pattern you are asking to be removed. State it specifically and in the present tense. For example: *When I hear my inner critic . . .*

2. *Acknowledge your reliance*

   In the second line, place your needs and concerns in the arms of the Universe, the care of God as you understand God. For example: *I vow with all living beings . . .*

3. *Let go of the old*

   Next, state your desire to let go of the root cause of your old behavior. For example: *To let go of self-doubt . . .*

4. *Invite in the new*

   Finally, state your aspiration for the virtue or characteristic you would like to cultivate in its place. For example: *And relish in being.*

✤ ✤ ✤

Examples of Vows

The following are examples of vows written in gāthā verse by participants in a class at Mind Roads Meditation Center.

> When I walk into the shadow of my shame,
> I vow with all living beings,
> To let go of my urge to hurt myself and the things around me
> And believe in my abiding beauty.

> When I am overcommitted and think I have to do more and
>   work harder,
> I vow with all living beings,
> To let go of doing
> And relish in being.

When I feel my jaw clenching,
I vow with all beings,
To stop the squashing
And feel my feelings fully.

When life feels too hard,
I vow with all living beings,
To let go of doubt and fear
And dwell in compassion for the benefit of all beings.

When I overeat and then hate myself,
I vow with the help of Buddha's love,
To feel the energy that is beneath the urge to eat
And stay with it.

When I feel the urge to withdraw,
I vow with all of creation,
To let go of self-hate and loathing,
And extend loving kindness to myself.

When I fear abandonment,
I vow with all living beings,
To stop and notice
And open to trust and love.

When I believe that I can and must fix everyone and everything,
I vow with all living beings,
To let go of carrying responsibility that is not mine
And trust that people and events will unfold as they will.

When I feel worthless,
I vow with all living beings,
To deny the lie (the illusion)
And rest in the joy of my true nature.

❖ ❖ ❖

Mindfulness Practice for Step Seven:
Write a Personal Vow

Vows catalyze the process of personal transformation. We aspire to awaken our better self, to water the seeds of our buddha nature so it may bloom. We call upon help from all living beings, sending tremors through Indra's great web of interbeing. And those tremors reverberate back to us. Knowing this to be true is the miracle of awakening.

In that spirit, write a personal vow for one of the shortcomings you would like to have transformed. Gently experiment with the four-line form of a gāthā verse as explained in the preceding pages.

1. *Open*

   In the first line, describe the shortcoming or habit-pattern you wish to release:

   When I

   _____

   For example:

   When I hear my inner critic . . .

   When I go into shame . . .

   When I want to eat . . .

   When I put myself last . . .

   When I get scared about money . . .

   When I procrastinate . . .

2. *Acknowledge your reliance*

   In the second line, place your needs and concerns in the arms of the Universe, the care of God as you understand God:

   I vow, with the help of

   _____

   For example:

   I vow with the help of my Higher Power . . .

   I vow with the help of all living beings . . .

(or you may wish to use alternate phrasing:)

Trusting in God, I ask . . .

Listening for guidance, I open to . . .

Entrusting myself to the Way, I vow . . .

3. *Let go of the old*

   In the third line, describe the root delusion or belief that fuels your pattern—what you need to release in order to open to something new:

   To let go of

   _____

   For example:

   To let go of self-doubt . . .

   To let go of self-reliance and mental worry . . .

   To let go of carrying responsibility that is not mine . . .

4. *Invite in the new*

   In the fourth and last line, describe what you want to cultivate in place of the shortcoming:

   And

   _____

   For example:

   And extend loving kindness to myself.

   And relish in being.

   And feel my feelings fully.

   And rest in the joy of my true nature.

   And receive the support of the Universe.

   And accept that all beings are the owners of their own karma.

   And open my heart, breathing in lasting comfort.

   ❖ ❖ ❖

Work with your gāthā verse. Memorize it. Write it down and put it in a book you read daily or place it next to your meditation cushion or chair. Turn your vow over in your mind during your meditation or morning quiet time. Let it soak into your consciousness. Hold your aspiration in your mind, especially the last line, all through the next year. Over the next weeks or months, observe what happens.

8

Finding Pearls in the Dust-Bin

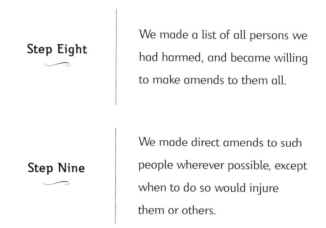

Step Eight

We made a list of all persons we had harmed, and became willing to make amends to them all.

Step Nine

We made direct amends to such people wherever possible, except when to do so would injure them or others.

MY MOTHER'S HEALTH took a steep decline when she reached her eighties. She was declared legally blind from macular degeneration and was confined to a wheelchair due to a series of strokes. Since she could no longer walk or see, we needed to move her out of her home of fifty years and into an assisted living apartment.

My sister Anne and I and our husbands arrived, vacuum cleaner and boxes of trash bags in hand. A teal-blue globe lamp still hung on a chain from the ceiling in my childhood bedroom, rusty-brown shag carpet covered a beautiful oak floor, and the hallway closet held paper napkins for every possible occasion. An antique dealer surveyed the rooms for saleable goods, loading her black Jeep with treasures.

I was sorting through piles of things in the "recreation room." My father and uncles had squared off half of the basement, paneling the walls in knotty pine and covering the floor with red and white linoleum tiles. It was our childhood playroom. Over to one side stood the entertainment bar, my father's favorite hangout.

On a shelf behind the bar, under a stack of loose papers and other miscellaneous junk, I found a small, dark-blue, bound copy of *Twelve Steps and Twelve Traditions*. It must have been sitting there all twenty years since my father died, right by where he used to stash his liquor bottles. He probably got it during one of his ten times in treatment. It was dated Thanksgiving, November 28, 1974, with a handwritten note tucked inside, "Hope you're feeling better, Joe." Someone from one of his AA groups must have given it to him.

Seeing his name scrawled in his own jagged, hard-to-read handwriting gave my body a jolt. *My God, he must have actually* read *this book. Who would have known?* As I thumbed through the volume, a multicolored card tumbled out from between the pages. It was a gold-gilded, Catholic holy card, a memento from his sister Mary's funeral in 1976.

Mostly, I was relieved when my father died: *I don't have to try to have a relationship with you anymore. I don't have to hurt anymore that you are destroying yourself and making our lives hell.* Over the years, I had done a lot of work in meditation regarding my father. One summer, I participated in a meditation intensive that focused on compassion. We followed an ancient Buddhist protocol of reflecting on our life one stage at a time, developing deeper understanding for the causes and conditions of our path. We started with looking at ourselves as a baby, then a five-year-old, then a ten-year-old, and on through our life span. After looking at ourselves, we meditated on our mother, going through the stages of her life and identifying significant influences. Next, we meditated on our father, considering the host of causes and conditions that shaped him.

While meditating on my father, imagining him as a five-year-old boy, I imagined him as the son of dirt-poor, illiterate, Irish-immigrant parents. *Did you feel embarrassed that they couldn't read, Dad? Did you cringe in the face of their old-world ways?* I thought about how *his* father was alcoholic, violent, and mean. (At least that's what everyone, except my father, said.)

Were you scared of him, like I was of you? I visualized him as the oldest boy in the family, stepping in to protect his mother, enlisting in the military during World War II, serving on the front lines in Northern Africa fighting against Mussolini. *Is that why you screamed in the night? Never let us watch war movies on TV?*

The meditations didn't erase the hurts of my childhood. I still don't think how he acted was okay. His rampages caused great harm to his family and friends. But my heart softened. I could imagine him as once a vulnerable boy, struggling. Barely eighteen, fighting for his life, witnessing his buddies dying in a foxhole in the African desert. I could feel sadness for him, see him as a tortured being—more than the big, mean man whom I loved and hated when I was a girl.

I studied the faded note in his *Twelve Steps and Twelve Traditions:* "Hope you're feeling better, Joe." *Who wrote you this, Dad? Your sponsor?* I realized he had friends in the Twelve Step program who hoped for his well-being. A great stream of recovering people had come before us, including AA members who reached out to my father five decades ago. They were the people who came to our home, drank coffee at the red Formica kitchen table, and urged him to go back to Twelve Step meetings.

Hearing them talk, wishing my father could be nice like them, had made me more open to reaching out for help when it was my turn to need it. Now grown-up and standing in the basement of my childhood home, I felt tender toward my father—sad that his demons ruled him, but glad he had tried to recover. Even if his attempts at getting sober were short-lived, they were something. He hadn't crossed over into a solid sobriety, but I had. *Thanks, Dad. I'm trying to be the best of you. Some days are going better than others.*

Seeing Our Shadow, Ending Our Isolation

Accepting our own shadow self, the part of us that acts badly and makes mistakes, builds deeper compassion for others. They are like us; we are like them. The shadow is not something that only "those other people out there" possess. The seeds of hatred and harm are within us all. Personally, it was unsettling, to say the least, to realize that I could feel hatred strong enough to want to kill. *Moi? Excuse me?*

I felt flashes of pure rage and hatred toward my father when I was a girl, especially when he was violent with my mother or siblings. Had I been bigger, had one of his guns been nearby, I believe I could have picked it up and shot him. It's ugly, but true. I used drugs and smoked cigarettes to repress the fiery feelings that scared and horrified me about myself. Actually, in its own way, drug use was probably a better choice than acting out violence. But, of course, it carried a terrible price.

Seeds of ill will and darkness are within us, side by side with the seeds of our buddha nature. Particular conditions in our life, as in the lives of others, can cause them to take root. When we sit down to make a list of the people we have harmed, we see that we are just like our fellow humans. We have no ground for feeling uppity or deeming ourselves superior. The more honest we become, the more compassion we are able to feel.

When we make a list of all the people we have harmed, we come face-to-face with the reality that we, too, have amends to make. The founders of the Twelve Step program say we should "ransack [our] memory for the people to whom we have given offense." And, if "our pencil falters, we can fortify and cheer ourselves by remembering what the A.A. experience in this Step has meant to others."[1] We can keep in mind that our ancestors in the Twelve Step program and in the traditions of spiritual practice were once like us. At the moment we falter, we can call on the many buddhas and spiritual seekers of old for strength or comfort. If we want to run, avoiding direct responsibility for what we have done or what we have failed to do, we are reminded of the promise of Step One that if we call out in our fear, we will "never fail to receive profound help."[2]

We can think of how we are the ancestors of others yet to come. Our recovery could become a source of hope, inspiration for a life of happiness and gratitude. Maybe one of these daughters or sons will find a note in our *Twelve Steps and Twelve Traditions* book and know they are not alone. Perhaps they, too, will be amazed to discover the possibility of joy arising from their suffering. The Buddhist saint Shantideva, in the *Bodhicharyavatara*, described such a realization like this:

As a blind man feels
when he finds a pearl in the dust-bin,

SO AM I AMAZED BY THE MIRACLE

OF AWAKENING

RISING IN MY CONSCIOUSNESS . . .

IT IS THE FEAST OF JOY

TO WHICH ALL ARE INVITED.[3]

❖ ❖ ❖

Early in recovery, I stubbornly held on to a delusion that my addiction hurt no one but myself. I was *not* my father. Since I was a closet drug user, most people didn't realize I was in trouble with amphetamines and other medications. I was numbed out, not home inside myself, and dissociated from my body. Most of my lies were from omission, not saying what was on my mind; I was a chameleon changing colors to fit into what I imagined other people wanted me to be. I didn't realize that being checked out from life affected not only me but many others too. I lived as if no one could see me, and I believed myself. It was familiar. Like home.

In the *Twelve Steps and Twelve Traditions,* it says Step Eight is "the beginning of the end of isolation." When we see that our actions have impact on others, many times not in the ways we intended, our bubble of delusion is shattered. Even though making amends is usually uncomfortable, the process shows us that we are not alone. Reality isn't the world over there, with me being a little bump over on the side, alone, forever doomed. In truth, we are a jewel in the great web of Indra, a part of the great interbeing with all that lives. This awareness, in itself, eases the loneliness and "not belonging" endemic to addicts, alcoholics, and codependent people.

Just the Right Amount of Remorse

If making a list of all the people we have harmed evokes deep remorse, it can be likened to a wound that stings because it's starting to heal. The pain of seeing our failings is helpful, motivating us to lay down our defenses and take full responsibility for our deeds. In Step Eight, we admit, first to ourselves and then to another, what we have done or failed to do. We acknowledge the consequences of our acts. In Step Nine, we make direct amends wherever possible. And we seek to change our behavior going forward. Traditional religious language refers to this process as "repenting" and "atoning" for the harm we have caused.

At first, the words *repent* and *atone* were off-putting. They raised ghosts of my Catholic past, conjuring images of a fierce, hairy John the Baptist rattling bones and breathing fire. I could feel the claustrophobia of kneeling in a dark confessional, wriggling with guilt, skin itching with shame. But holding the words *repent* and *atone* in meditation has unveiled their deeper meanings, like a series of nested Russian dolls revealing delight after delight.

The practice of repenting and atoning, as suggested by Step Eight, has been going on for more than twenty-five hundred years. In the Buddhist view, traits such as greed, anger, and ignorance are realities of human life. They rise endlessly. Not only weak, bad, or addicted people struggle with them. All people struggle with them. (Remember, in the first of Buddha's Four Pure Insights on the Way Things Are, that suffering, or *dukkha,* is inescapable.)

Human failings and their consequences, the accumulation of karma in our lifetime, are simply matter-of-fact, nothing unusual or special. The more important question is: What are we going to do about it? We need ways to unburden the negative karma we accumulate. The way to become free is to repent and atone. Make a list and become willing to make amends to all the people we have harmed. Many generations before us bear witness to the importance and value of atoning for injury we have caused. When we make amends for our wrongs, take responsibility for our karma, our burden of shame is lightened.

But first, to become willing, we need to feel remorse. Just the right amount of remorse is called for: not too much and not too little. This is similar to the instructions for how to sit in meditation. We are told to keep our body alert and yet relaxed, not too loose and not too tight. Neither falling asleep nor worrying too much.

If we have *too little* remorse, denying our responsibility in causing harm, we are being too loose with ourselves. There may be things in our shadow we don't want to see because the qualities don't fit with our image of our self. We defend our self from that knowledge with denial or naïveté.

Step Eight invites us to strip off the armor of our denial, to let go of rationalizing, justifying, or blaming others for our actions. To stop nursing thoughts such as, *Well, you should have seen what* they *did.* Efforts to protect ourselves from getting hurt are often at the root of actions that cause harm to others. If we hide in "purposeful forgetting," deny our shadow, and defend our unskillful acts, we stay trapped.[4] Inside, we are shameful, alone, and unforgiven.

On the other hand, we don't want to get mired down in *too much* remorse. Drowning in regret can be compared to being too tight on the meditation cushion. We exaggerate our faults, taking on responsibility that is not ours. When absorbed in our own guilt and shame, our world shrinks. It gets filled up with *Me!* Being preoccupied with our faults, continually evaluating our behaviors or ruthlessly criticizing our mistakes eats up our attention. Anxious or depressed feelings dominate our emotional landscape. Too much remorse is not much better than too little. In either case, we are unable to be present in our relationships or in life.

What we need is "just the right amount of remorse to be transformative."[5] If we can feel both sorrow for the hurts we have caused and—at the same time, in the same breath—accept ourselves the way we are, then our remorse inspires change. Just the right amount does not drown us in regret or humiliate us in shame. An underlying kindness and acceptance of ourselves is necessary if we are going to make an honest list of the people we have harmed. If we aren't afraid of our shadow, we don't have to wall ourselves off with defenses; we can open our heart. Imagine the possibility of a new way of being in the world.

Being mindful of our remorse helps us find the sweet spot of "just enough." We can notice when we are blaming others and the sensations related to that mind-set in our body and heart. *Oops—feeling "done to."* *What's my part here?* If we are spiraling down in shame, withdrawing, or feeding toxic thoughts, we can pull ourselves back. *Oops—going down.* *Need some loving kindness here. Everyone makes mistakes.* If there is an imbalance of too much or too little remorse, mindful awareness brings us back to center, the point of "just enough" remorse.

I am comforted by imagining generations of people repenting and atoning for their wrongs. I am merely one of multitudes. Tenshin-roshi Reb Anderson says:

> Bodhisattvas continually see and admit their own delusions
> and nonvirtuous deeds. Less enlightened people confess less
> often. The most unenlightened and dangerous people are
> those who think they never do any nonvirtuous deeds at all.
> The greatest darkness of the human mind is to believe that
> you never do anything wrong or hurtful or stupid . . .
> Confession of wrong-doing is an act of awakening.[6]

◈   ◈   ◈

There is great freedom in joining the stream of humanness, knowing we are like all others, both good and bad. We admit we are just an ordinary person, doing our best, which is sometimes great and other times not so hot. We can relax about it.

Starting with the Smallest Desire to Make Amends

Some years ago my husband Jim and I went to a Zen retreat (sesshin) at the Minnesota Zen Meditation Center with visiting teacher Tenshin-roshi Reb Anderson from San Francisco. He talked about the strong tradition of repentance and atoning in Buddhism. In the early days, Buddha had very few rituals (unlike most religions now), no bowing, chanting, or wearing ankle-length black robes. The only ritual he adhered to was inviting his disciples "to come forth," to have an authentic encounter with him. Tell the truth about your struggles, failings, or hindrances to practice.

Tenshin-roshi invited us to come up and confess our struggles and failings. He sat, dignified and erect, wrapped in steel-blue robes, seated in the lotus position. On the carved cedar mantle behind him, incense burned. Orange gladioli and yellow mums in a Ceylon porcelain vase framed an image of Buddha. A large rectangular cushion *(zabuton)* had been placed in front of Tenshin-roshi, gracing the polished oak floor of the Zen center. It held a smaller round black cushion stuffed with barley seeds, called a *zafu*.

He looked out at us all with piercing, vibrant eyes and said, "So come forth."

Any participant could come up to the front of the room, sit in front of Tenshin-roshi, and ask a question or talk about his or her struggles. We were invited to confess our shortcomings while held in the loving attention of the community of participants. I found the rigorous honesty of people who came forth to be quite moving. The stories varied, but the human struggles within them echoed each other.

A seventysomething man approached the empty cushion.

After bowing first to Tenshin-roshi and then to the group, he sat down. He confessed his disillusionment and fury with the current Congress and administration of the United States.

"When I read the morning newspaper, see story after story of lies, corruption, and war, I get angry. Our government is responsible. We are *all* responsible. Our leaders don't admit the mess we're in. It's like they live on a different planet. I am so pissed off I can hardly stand it. What can I do with this feeling of hate?"

Tenshin-roshi nodded.

"Of course. Part of what makes the current situation in the world so scary is that there are deluded people who also have great power. It's important to understand the nature of power, which is to corrupt. If you can understand the nature of power as a corrupting force, does your feeling shift? Do you want to have any compassion?"

"Yeah, I'd *like* to be able to have compassion. I just don't at the moment."

Smiling, Tenshin-roshi said, "Well, that's a good start."

The exchange reminded me of the counsel given in the Twelve Step program when we are told that a "desire to desire" to make amends is good enough. Even a desire to desire opens the heart. The grace of loving kindness can get in when the soft spot in our heart is undefended. We can experience compassion and joy.

Making Direct Amends Wherever Possible

These ideas are all great in theory, but sometimes when we offer our amends, it doesn't go all that well. The other person may not be forgiving. They may stay angry, hurt, or determined to blame.

THE CLASS SESSION WAS DUE TO START in little over an hour. My colleague and I were co-facilitating and had agreed to meet early that morning to finish our preparations. I had already been waiting for forty-five minutes. No colleague. When I called my voice mail, there was no message. I was getting steamed.

I was counting on her, this time of all times. Over the past few days, there had been another medical emergency with my elderly, dying mother. The situation required all my attention, leaving no time to prepare for the class.

When I'd called my colleague the day before, she said, "Don't worry about a thing. An e-mail with all the materials for the class will be waiting for you tonight when you get home. I am happy to carry the load. It's the least I can do."

Indeed, when I checked my e-mail late that evening, there was a note from her. The attached document was four pages of stream-of-consciousness, random thoughts about the topic for the session. There was nothing close to a class plan.

When she finally walked in, I was cold. "You're late! People will be coming soon and we aren't ready. What happened?"

She burst into tears. "I called and left a message a little while ago. Didn't you check? I couldn't get going this morning, so I stayed home to have a second cup of coffee. Then there was construction on the freeway. Besides, I sent you an e-mail yesterday with all the stuff."

"We're nowhere *near* ready for the class. I couldn't follow what you sent. I was counting on you."

She cried louder, looked down, and collapsed in a heap on the floor. She then gave a big sigh, putting the back of her hand to her forehead.

I blew up, yelling, "What are you doing? You've got to be kidding me. You're the one who was late! We don't have time for this; we need to get organized."

Somehow we managed to talk about the plan and teach a respectable class, but it was tough. I was very angry, and my colleague wouldn't look at me. I'm sure the participants could sense the tension.

After the session was over, I told her I was sorry I had gotten so angry and wished I could have handled it better. I said I was anxious and exhausted after being with my mother and had been relying on her to have everything ready. Nonetheless, I shouldn't have yelled at her. I asked her to forgive me if I had hurt her, as appeared to be the case.

She said, "Thank you for the apology." Then she got out the door as fast as she could. Not a peep about her part, nothing about her own responsibility in the matter.

Over the following weeks, she called several mutual acquaintances, telling them how touchy and difficult to work with I was. One of our mutual friends told me about these conversations a few months later. I got mad all over again.

While meditating, I eventually saw there was hurt beneath my angry feelings. I had counted on her to carry the ball and she hadn't. I apologized and she didn't accept the amends. And then she spoke ill of me to others. Even so, I had gotten angry to cover the hurt and let myself run with it. No matter what, I was completely responsible for how I behaved with her.

At my invitation, we met for coffee. I went over the incident again, telling her how much I had been depending on her. I apologized again for blowing up. I told her I was hurt to learn that she talked with others, saying disparaging things. I wished she would have come to me directly if she was still upset.

My colleague listened politely, saying she appreciated my apology. But she took no responsibility for her part in what happened, holding to the view that she was innocent, I was mean, and she had been "done to." I was disappointed in her response, but content with my efforts to make amends. Despite how it had gone between us, I could be at peace.

ONCE WE HAVE ATONED for our wrongs—even if the other person is not inclined to forgive us, even if this person is not willing to own his or her part in the difficulty—we need to let go. Accept that there is nothing more to do. We can experience the relief of having no secrets, making no excuses, and holding no pretenses. We can feel the satisfaction that we have done Step Nine and "made direct amends to such people wherever possible." Here we experience the freedom of taking care of our emotional business.

We don't have to feel the weight of old guilt or live with the fear of running into someone we have harmed. We don't have the worry: *Jeez, I hope I don't ever see so-and-so because I won't be able to look her in the eye. I'm so humiliated when I think of how I acted. I want to run the other way.* Nor do we have the burden of procrastination weighing us down: *I've had this person's name on my amends list for the last five years, and I'm still getting ready.* We simply take care of what we can "as fast and as far as may be possible."[7]

Buddha referred to this inner satisfaction as the "bliss of blamelessness."[8] Certainly, most of us will err again, despite our good intentions. But there is happiness in taking full responsibility. Not blaming others. Not absorbing blame from others. Being free from shame. Tenshin-roshi Reb Anderson says, "Admitting who you are, you are purified. Being purified, you can now go home to awakening."[9]

Making Amends by Speaking Up

Another type of amends involves speaking up and saying the things we have never dared to say. Some people raised in alcoholic or addictive families have learned it isn't safe to speak up about their feelings and needs. They have been dismissed, demeaned, or even abused. And yet indirectness or withholding can be hurtful too. We can continue to hide our feelings, carrying the belief that we are "unsafe" into relationships where it is not true.

MY CLIENT AMY DIDN'T WANT TO HURT HER DAD. He had been through so much grief with her mother's drinking before they divorced. Instead of telling him she felt stung by his criticisms—angry and hurt— she tried to just act pleasant, make like everything was fine. For years.

Amy and her dad met for lunch one summer afternoon; he called and invited her. Sitting at a table outside under the patio umbrella, munching on fresh lettuce and tomato salad, Amy got a surprise. Her father brought up how she seemed distant, hadn't called much, hadn't dropped by for a visit, and seemed preoccupied and in a hurry when they did talk.

"Is anything bothering you, Amy? Are you mad at me about something?"

"No, no, nothing, Dad."

"Are you sure? If you are upset with me, I really want you to tell me."

"No, no, everything's fine."

"I want to have a good relationship with you, Amy. You are so very important to me. I really have the feeling something's on your mind. I can take it; just tell me."

"Weeell, there was that time last fall when you criticized me for letting Sophie stay at Mom's for the weekend. And that cranky e-mail you sent me when I moved, telling me you were annoyed because I didn't have a new phone yet. I knew you weren't happy with me. I *always* know. Sometimes I think you expect me to be perfect."

Her father said he hadn't meant to be critical. He thought he was just commenting. He confessed that his (now) wife had given him similar feedback, saying almost those exact words, "I feel like you expect me to be perfect." He hadn't been aware of this habit in himself until now.

"I'll try to watch it, Amy. But I need you to tell me if I've hurt you, not just become distant. I love you."

As AMY TOLD ME about their lunchtime conversation, she realized she had hurt her father by trying *not* to hurt him, by keeping her feelings to herself. It shocked her. She was equally surprised at how well her father took her feedback. He wasn't as fragile as she thought he was. In fact, he wasn't the least bit brittle. Although their conversation had been intense, it brought them closer.

Sometimes being "nice" isn't very nice. Our feelings of anger or hurt leak anyway. Maybe our jokes have an edge, we withdraw from the relationship, or we speak ill of the other person behind his or her back. By acting in codependent ways, we can do harm, both to ourselves and our relationships. In this case, making amends involves being more emotionally honest with a person we love.

Experiencing the Grace of Forgiveness

Still other times, making amends can be a comforting experience. In *Twelve Steps and Twelve Traditions*, it says, "The generous response of most people to such . . . sincerity will often astonish us. Even our severest and most justified critics will frequently meet us more than halfway."[10]

Before being with my husband, Jim, I knew very little of the joy of being forgiven. I kept striving to be "good," constantly anxious because it was impossible. In my family growing up, people didn't talk out their problems. They cut off relationships, didn't speak for years. Consequently, making a mistake was scary. The world seemed threatening and unsafe.

But with Jim, when I ask for his forgiveness after being difficult in some way, he never fails to give it. He smiles his shy smile and says, "It's in the past." He actually *means* it. After these thirty years of our life together, I am much more relaxed about my mistakes. Jim says it took the first fifteen years for me to trust he wouldn't get angry and abandon me. Now, the fear held in the very cells of my body has nearly gone.

Through the grace of others' forgiveness, perhaps we can, at last, abandon perfectionism. In the words of Tenshin-roshi Reb Anderson:

> WHEN I ADMIT THAT I AM JUST AS I AM,
> I ALLOW MYSELF TO BE SO . . .
> BUDDHA'S COMPASSION EMBRACES ME
> JUST AS I AM RIGHT HERE AND NOW,
> WITH THE PURITY OF COMPLETE FORGIVENESS.[11]

❖ ❖ ❖

Mindfulness Practice for Steps Eight and Nine

In Buddhism, at the end of our meditation period each morning—at home or in a practice center—we are advised to chant the following prayer of atonement:

> ALL MY ANCIENT TWISTED KARMA
> FROM BEGINNINGLESS GREED,
> HATE, AND DELUSION,
> BORN THROUGH BODY, SPEECH, AND MIND,
> I NOW FULLY AVOW.[12]

(Say three times, bowing with each recitation.)

❖ ❖ ❖

This daily mindfulness practice keeps us from being seduced back into our delusions of denial or exaggerated fault. We stay aware of the endless nature of the human struggle. We join the great stream of many, through thousands of years, atoning for their failings, lightening the burden of their accumulated karma. Although this prayer was at first a bit forbidding, I now cherish this time-tested practice of repentance. I have experienced relief and freedom from shame, moments of touching the bliss of blame-lessness—surprisingly, right in the middle of the muck.

9

Standing on the Ground of Our Deeds

| **Step Ten** | We continued to take personal inventory and when we were wrong promptly admitted it. |

EVEN BUDDHA'S SON had hassles with his dad.

In the ancient tale, "Advice to Rāhula," Gautama Buddha is unhappy with his son, Rāhula, for lying to his other kid pals while playing tag in the forest. Buddha calls Rāhula over to his side, admonishing him for his actions. In a stern voice, Buddha tells him that "anyone who feels no shame in telling a deliberate lie" is headed for sure trouble.[1] If a lie is told, even in jest, it opens the door for other harmful deeds. Those can be rationalized away too. As a countermeasure, Buddha-the-dad instructs Rāhula to constantly reflect on his thoughts, words, and actions. Make it a habit, he advises:

> "Thus, Rāhula, you should train yourself, 'I will not tell a deliberate lie even in jest.' How do you construe this, Rāhula: What is a mirror for?"
>
> "For reflection, sir."
>
> "In the same way, Rāhula, physical acts, verbal acts, and mental acts are to be done with repeated reflection."[2]

Three Times to Reflect on Our Actions

By suggesting an ongoing personal inventory, Step Ten counsels us to repeatedly hold a mirror up to our thoughts and actions. In fact, the Buddha said, there are three times we should reflect on our actions: before, during, and after we do something. (I'd say that about covers it.) Reflection helps us to "purify our destructive habits" of body, speech, and mind.[3]

If we fail to reflect, we stay unaware. Our old habits rule. They become our normal way of doing life, a mental and neurological default. In the throes of our addiction we were anything but cognizant, blurred by drugs and alcohol—or (pick your "fix" of choice) sex, food, gambling, shopping, or the craving for love. Without mindful awareness before, during, and after our actions, we don't have an iota of a chance for a better life. The age-old teachings of Buddhism encourage reflection, and Step Ten tells us to make it a regular habit.

Reflecting on Our Actions after the Fact

Many people in recovery tell me that, *if* they are reflecting on their actions at all, it is usually after the fact. Never mind before or during—being *that* aware seems nearly out of reach. But reflecting after the fact is still valuable. It may inspire just the right amount of remorse, enough for us to change our ways.

Now we refer to it as "The Great Christmas Brownie Episode." Early in my recovery, I found the Christmas season especially difficult. It's still not my favorite time of year. Maybe it's the long hours of darkness in my region of the world, or the history of drinking and tension in my family growing up, or memories of the despair that led to attempting suicide as a teen. Something rumbles in my psyche—painful personal history colliding with society's expectation of "fa-la-la."

We were supposed to bring homemade goodies to the Christmas Eve party at the Newman Center. Fresh-baked brownies, crowned in rich, gooey, homemade chocolate frosting sat on the countertop, still in their silver baking pan. Next to them lay my grandmother's cut-glass cookie plate, lined with lacy white paper doilies. I loved making things look beautiful, including food for the festivities. It was Christmas and everything had to be just so. It had always been that way.

Upstairs in the bathroom, I was drying my hair, finishing the final touches on my makeup and clothes. It was time to leave, and I was still rushing around. My husband, Jim, always one to be on time, had been ready for at least ten minutes. He came upstairs and started pacing the hall.

"It's time to go, hon. Are you ready?"

I turned the dryer off.

"Whaaat?"

"Let's get going. We're going to be late."

"Oh no! I'll be ready in a minute. But I haven't cut the brownies yet."

"Can I do it? We're going to be late."

"Yeah, great. All the stuff is right there. I'll be down in a jiff."

When I walked into the kitchen a few minutes later, he had most of the brownies cut, in a whole variety of sizes: big, medium-big, small, medium-small, and bite-size. Some were cut even, some were jagged-edged.

"Nooo! Jim, those brownies don't look right. They're supposed to be the same size so they'll look nice on the plate!"

"What difference does it make? They're perfectly fine!"

"No, they're not! I went to all this trouble and now they're a mess. I'll finish them."

"*Fine.* You don't like how I do it, *fine.* Help yourself. Who cares what they look like anyway? They're supposed to taste good, not look like they came out of a magazine."

"*I* care."

I felt tension building: knotted-up stomach, fatigued brain, and a short fuse. Too many hours had been spent exchanging gifts and smiling in good cheer.

"Well, hurry up. We're late."

"Stop pressuring me! I'll show you what we can do with these blasted brownies—*this!*"

We stood there staring at each other, speechless.

Chocolate goo covered half the kitchen floor. It took us fifteen minutes to clean up the mess. We arrived at the party late and empty-handed.

THE GOOD AND BAD NEWS about reflecting on our actions after the fact is that we may have a mess to clean up. In the car on the way to the festivities,

I admitted I was wrong and made amends to Jim for letting my stress boil over. Jim was forgiving, recognizing that he added fuel to the fire with his impatience. I felt surprised and embarrassed, unaware that I was *that* on edge, and horrified at myself for throwing food on the floor. I was glad to be able to take responsibility for my behavior—to notice, once again, that perfectionism is not my friend.

Going forward, I could see that the holiday season evokes more grief and stress than I wanted to admit. A lovely plate of cookies and gifts wrapped ever-so-beautifully isn't going to fix the pain of my past. As is true for many codependent people, I needed to make taking care of myself a higher priority and stay more mindful of the signs of pressure building up.

I am happy to say that I have never pitched another pan of brownies in unabated frustration. The episode remains a source of much laughter in the family—and an icon of the need for mindfulness while under stress.

When teaching about the need to reflect on our actions after the fact, Buddha said:

> Having performed a [physical] act, you should reflect on it . . .
> If, on reflection, you know that it led to [harm toward self or others], then you should confess it, reveal it, and lay it open to a knowledgeable companion in the holy life. Having confessed it . . . you should exercise restraint in the future.
>
> But if on reflection you know that it did not lead to affliction . . . then you should stay mentally refreshed and joyful, training day and night in skillful mental qualities.[4]

❖ ❖ ❖

Reflecting on Our Actions Midstream

Buddha also suggests that we reflect in the midst of acting or reacting, right as we are saying or doing something. The writers of *Twelve Steps and Twelve Traditions* call this taking "a "spot-check inventory.""[5]

Here our mindfulness practice comes in handy. On the cushion, we train ourselves to observe our sensations, thoughts, and feelings. We sit with them, letting whatever arises pass on through. In Step Ten we become ready to take these skills off the cushion and into everyday life. We just notice, without acting out (harming others) or acting in (harming ourselves).

For example, while talking to our friend or family member, we can take a spot check. Just notice: *What am I feeling in my body right now? What is the tone of my voice? How does the conversation seem to be going? What is the effect on me or the other person? Is my action helping or hurting?*

The habit of spot-checking during the day can be practiced randomly, in the midst of any interaction or whenever a toxic body sensation, thought pattern, or emotional state alerts our attention. A spot check acts like an inner mindfulness bell, signaling us: *Whoa! Time out . . . Take a breath here.* By stopping and breathing, we interrupt chain reactions of thoughts, feelings, and knee-jerk behaviors. We can short-circuit an unskillful action before we have a mess to clean up.

But this is not possible if we lecture, scold, or call ourselves names. We need to bring the same nonjudging, nonblaming attitude that we have on the meditation cushion to our spot-check inventory. We observe ourselves in the moment with the "bare awareness" we use when watching our breath. During the momentary pause between breathing out and breathing in, the kind teacher within us can say, *You* could *do that—but maybe not.* We can breathe consciously, letting it soothe us on the spot, using this time-honored, simple practice taught by Thích Nhất Hanh:

> On the first breath, silently say to yourself, "I breathe *in,* experiencing habitual patterns of mind. I breathe *out,* experiencing habitual states of mind."
>
> Stay with this for several more in-breaths and out-breaths, silently repeating, "States of mind."
>
> On the next breath, silently say to yourself, "I breathe *in, calming* habitual patterns of mind. I breathe *out,* calming habitual states of mind."
>
> Stay with this for several more in-breaths and out-breaths, silently repeating, "Calming myself."[6]

❖ ❖ ❖

Why does breath awareness and meditation help us regulate our reactions? Because, as mentioned earlier, it changes the very chemistry and structure of the brain. In doing Step Ten, we draw on the resources of the left prefrontal lobe, which helps us temper impulsivity, calm negative emotions, and rein in reactivity. The effect is like a physiological pause button that slows down our knee-jerk responses of anger or self-destruction. Research indicates that this area of the brain can become more active after just eight weeks of mindfulness training.[7]

Reflecting before We Act

In addition, ongoing meditation practice creates more neural pathways from the executive center of the brain to the emotional part of the brain. Signals to "calm down" reach our emotional brain faster. We have a better chance of catching ourselves *before* going down a destructive path of self-loathing, self-destruction, or compulsive acts.

JIM WAS DRIVING THE CAR AND TURNED WEST ON HIGHWAY 5 as we made our way to my parents' house for a holiday dinner. After the infamous brownie episode, we started anticipating the stress of these family visits and made a point of talking about how we were doing before the fact.

"So how are you doing, hon?"

"Crabby," I said. "Could you turn the radio down, please? I hate these endless Christmas tunes."

"Me too. Visiting your family is difficult, and I didn't even grow up there. So how are you, really?"

"Sad there's so much pain in my family and I can't fix it. Scared, because my father could turn sarcastic and mean at the drop of a hat, especially if he has been drinking, which he hasn't for a while now, but you never know. Everyone acts like nothing is happening, like we are all one happy bunch. My stomach is all knotted up. I feel invisible when I am with them, and that feeling is so old and familiar. No one will ask a thing about our life. Sometimes, I could sob."

Jim reached over and clasped my hand.

"I know," he said.

I focused in on the sensations of the warmth of his hand on mine, the soft pulse of his heartbeat through his skin to mine, breathing in, coming to the present moment of being in the car with Jim. *I know he is here for me. Here and now.*

We started thinking and talking about the many friends in our community of loved ones, naming them aloud.

My family's suffering was only a part of my life. Breathing in, I began thinking of all the other people who have pain in their alcoholic families at this time of year, at this moment. Breathing out, I sent them loving kindness, feeling connected to others with similar difficulties. It's not just my suffering; it's the suffering of all. And the happiness for some people at this time of year is not just their happiness; it's the happiness. We are interbeing.

In the car, driving along the icy, salted highway under the gray overcast sky, Jim and I sent mental wishes of goodwill and loving kindness to our loved ones as each one came to mind. Then we listed topics we could bring up at the dinner table and made a bet about how many times we could get the word *egregious* into casual conversation. We started laughing at some of the outrageous possibilities.

Jim glanced over, "Two hours max, right?"

"Deal."

We actually had a pretty good time. There was sorrow afterward, of course, including grief about how alcoholism has devoured my family. And there was gratitude for being in recovery.

ONGOING MINDFULNESS helps us notice the pressure in our chest, the hairs rising on our neck, or the toxic thoughts that precede an emotional hijack. We can catch the early warning signs, cautions that a reaction is in the works: *Here it comes!* or *When I feel like this I just don't care.* We can do this before we act *out* an impulse (explode in anger, make a barbed joke, skip out on our Twelve Step meeting) or act it *in* (eat a carton of ice cream, go to bed depressed, mercilessly criticize ourselves).

Regular on-the-spot checks—before, during, or after our actions—help us have fewer emotional or relationship messes to clean up. We can short-circuit our reactions, before the neuronal impulses travel down the well-worn tracks of our emotional brain. We can gain greater peace of mind when taking full responsibility for our actions. We are more free to choose how we want to be in the world, liberated from the toxicity of our addictive mind. In the words of the Buddha, "This is how the sincere practice of mindfulness leads to a vast harvest and great richness."[8]

Taking an Evening Inventory with Naikan Practice

The founders of the Twelve Step program also suggest we incorporate an evening inventory into our routine "when we review the happenings of the hours just past."[9] This practice helps us stay in emotional balance.

As a tool for doing this inventory, I have come to love the practice of *Naikan,* Japanese for "looking inside." Naikan was developed in Japan in the 1940s by Ishin Yoshimoto, a Buddhist of the Pure Land sect *(Jodo Shinshu).* Dr. Yoshimoto practiced *mishirabe,* a rigorous and difficult method of meditation and self-reflection. He wanted to make the benefits of such practice accessible to more people, so he developed the more gentle Naikan practice.

Although less familiar to those of us living in the United States, Naikan is widely used in mental health centers and addiction treatment centers in Japan. More recently, it has been introduced to the West by Gregg Krech, in his book *Naikan: Gratitude, Grace, and the Japanese Art of Self-Reflection.*

Naikan offers a simple, beautiful way to take inventory. In essence, we reflect on the past twenty-four hours of our life and ask ourselves three simple but profound questions:

- What have I received?

- What have I given?

- What difficulties have I caused?

What Have I Received?

In Naikan practice, we train the mind in balance. Our mind develops "a wide-angle lens."[10] Starting an evening inventory with the first Naikan question shifts our attention away from the pain of our difficulties to the joys of what we have received. We move from the natural human tendency to zero in on what bothers and agitates us to seeing a more complete view. This is not to say that we revert to denial about things that are distressing and difficult. Rather, we learn to keep our troubles in perspective. We practice looking at the whole picture, both the good and the bad.

In a typical Naikan reflection, we think about what we have received in general in the past twenty-four hours. Other options are to reflect on what we have received from a particular relationship or a certain circumstance. Another useful option, especially early in our sobriety, is to pose the first question in this way: What have I received in the past twenty-four hours that supports my recovery?

Many of us who come from alcoholic families are "waiting for the other shoe to drop," anticipating disappointments, disasters, or both around the corner. It's hard to just stop and hold your heart open to what is in the moment—what is in this one day.

When I turned twenty-five, Marty Heist brought me flowers. He came to my office with a big bouquet of yellow daffodils and other symbols of spring.

In 1978, I got a job working for the Johnson Institute. Marty, the kind man who heard my first Fifth Step, was now a colleague. I was a little over three years into recovery when Marty and I went out to lunch for my birthday.

"I want you to put these flowers in fresh water, so they'll last. And every time you look at them, soak in a little bit more of my fondness and regard for you. Try to take in some of the positive energy I am sending you, because I know how hard it is for you to receive good things."

I was surprised he could see through me, but that was Marty. Although I was in recovery, deep down my heart remained guarded. People's care and the goodness of life bounced off, as if I were clothed in a rubberized suit. I did not trust goodness or joy. The moment something good happened, I felt afraid, anticipating that it would blow up and that something bad would be lurking right around the corner. Many of the happy times of my life, to that point, had gone south.

Marty planted a seed: *Oh, I should pause and soak in the good stuff.*

I did not discover Naikan for several more years, but it has been a powerful, mind-transforming practice. Taking a regular evening inventory, reflecting on what I have received time and time again, began to grow a deep appreciation for my life, a spontaneous gratitude. With the first question—*What have I received in the past twenty-four hours that supports my recovery?*—we pause to notice blessings.

In Naikan, blessings include big things such as the skills and the talents that we received at birth. They also include the small, nitty-gritty things we receive, such as the hot water in our shower, the coolness of the air conditioning in summer, the wonderful salad of fresh greens we had for dinner. Noticing such things is like making a gratitude list and making it very concrete. When we write down specific examples, we can't refute them.

We often take the "little" blessings for granted. But are these things really so little? Maybe they only appear so because our attention is elsewhere. We miss the ways we are supported, day-to-day, like the fact that our heart is beating, our legs are walking, and our lungs are breathing. These are the very things that keep us alive and aware.

Here are some personal examples of one day's reflections on the first Naikan question:

Hot water and mint-scented soap in the shower this morning

Rich, hot Colombian coffee for breakfast

My husband, Jim, who made homemade bread that we took to Jamie after his surgery, brought Chinese food home for dinner, kissed me good-night

My granddaughter's funny handmade drawings on the refrigerator door

The beautiful orchid plant blooming in the shower

Our flush toilets

The telephone that works

My warm navy-blue wool sweater to wear on today's cool day

My eyes that see, while my mother is blind

Being drug-free today

The Twelve Step fellowship to come home to

All those in recovery who have come before me, shown us the way

❖ ❖ ❖

Perhaps it is a surprise to think that reflecting on the small things we receive in life, including the ways we are supported in our sobriety, prepares us to "promptly admit" when we are wrong. But it does. If we can acknowledge and receive what we are given in each moment of life, then admitting when we err isn't so threatening. Mistakes and difficulties are only part of the big picture. During that same twenty-four hours, there may also be a breathtaking sunset and a wonderful kitty that curls up in your lap. There is clean air for you to breathe, a mindfulness practice for you to cultivate, and a Twelve Step meeting for you to join.

In traditional Naikan practice, the third question is considered the most important. I'm not sure I agree. The first question is also vital, especially for those of us with deeply internalized shame and adult-child-of-alcoholic identities. Realizing we are supported by the Great Reality of the Universe and other people in recovery creates the emotional safety needed to promptly admit when we are wrong.

What Have I Given?

Ah, now we start to consider what we have given back. This question is about the practical and spiritual reconciliation of our relationships with others. Does the world owe me, or do I owe the world?

We often live our lives as if the world owes us. *Why didn't I get that raise? Why is the pizza so late? Why am I not getting more appreciation from my boss?* Perhaps we feel resentment when other people let us down, not fulfilling our hopes or expectations. And when people *are* supportive, perhaps we take their efforts for granted, as if we were entitled to such efforts. An alternative that supports our recovery is to practice Step Ten, thinking about the second Naikan question and answering it in detail.

At one time I panicked before writing my answers to this question. I worried that I would not be able to come up with anything. But when I actually started writing, I realized, *Oh yeah, I did give something back. I said hello to the lady at the grocery store.* And that was just the beginning.

The founders of the Twelve Step program told us to consider all the small ways we contributed to a better world. AA literature notes that it is important to give ourselves credit for *any* way that we acted responsibly, any way we gave to others. This is especially important in early recovery. If you made your bed today, you did good. If you said hello to the bus driver, it counted. *Every* act of responsibility or kindness counts. This is what we recall in the second Naikan question, and it is of great value in taking the inventory suggested in Step Ten.

As with the first Naikan question, we can focus our reflections on a specific period of time: *What have I given back in the past twenty-four hours?* Following are examples from my reflections:

I thanked Jim for baking bread for Jamie yesterday.

I listened to Jim talk about his relationship with his son and offered my thoughts.

I watered my orchids and told them they were beautiful.

I smiled at the women in the tea shop and made friendly conversation.

I took my friend Jody to dinner to celebrate her birthday.

I fed the cats.

I knitted caps for my granddaughters.

I gave the talk at the Twelve Steps and Mindfulness meeting.

◈ ◈ ◈

Reflecting on the second Naikan question can yield several levels of insight. For me, it was interesting to realize that I *do* give back. I also found that I wanted to give more but had been neglecting some basic self-care. I needed to do a better job of feeding, exercising, and resting my body.

In addition, asking this question helps us to see distortions in our thinking about how we give to others. For example, people of the codependent persuasion may find they have an overly long list of what they have given. They've given and given and given—and perhaps are resentful as hell about it. They see they are not giving to themselves in ways that are sustaining, emotionally and spiritually. Other people in recovery may see that they actually give little to others. Seeing the truth of self-centeredness can sometimes spark a desire to change.

On a spiritual level, we see in the miracle of life that we can never repay what we have been given. We can only be struck with awe and gratitude at its mystery.

In a Naikan workshop, people read their reflections aloud. In clusters of three or four, one person reads while the others listen in "noble silence," without comment.[11] Listeners send the reader kindness in nonverbal ways, and people bow to each other at the end. The bow says in a physical way, *Thank you for sharing your practice with me. May you be well.* Attention then moves on to the next reader.

When I facilitate, I can hear snatches of what people are reading. As I sit in my seat, a symphony of human voices whispers as if in surround sound. The mindfulness bell rings regularly, beginning another round of reflection reading. Inevitably, as people speak their Naikan inventories, the energy in the room lightens. People often say they feel "grateful," "surprised," or "content." I get teary, touched by the bigness and loveliness of life—even a troubled life.

What Difficulties Have I Caused?

Implicit in this third Naikan question are many others: Do I give back to the Universe and to the earth and to the community? Do I realize that giving to others helps my own recovery and way of living? Am I willing to own up to the difficulties I cause, even if I didn't intend them? Am I willing to clean up my relationship messes, preferably each night before I sleep?

Following are some personal examples from one day's reflections on the third Naikan question, posed as: *What difficulties and troubles have I caused in the past twenty-four hours?*

> *I overreacted to Jim's comment, "Don't you already know how to put the collar back on that coat? Haven't you done it before?" I got irritated at his criticism. I pressed my point more than I needed to, indulged in staying angry even after Jim apologized.*

> *I was judgmental and complained about one of our renters.*

> *I neglected to write a sympathy card to Ruth for another week.*

> *I pressured myself to make things perfect for the company we have coming and turned into a bundle of tension.*

> *I didn't pay any attention to the cats today.*

I used a lot of paper towels.
I didn't turn all my lights off, left them burning.

✦ ✦ ✦

Notice that nowhere in Naikan practice do we reflect on what some-body else did to us or why we were justified in our reaction. Naikan is based on the principle of karma, which reminds us that our deeds are the ground upon which we stand. Every action of ours causes a corresponding effect. No choice or thought or behavior is exempt. We are sowing karma and reaping what we sow, for better or worse, in all that we think and do. As the *Upajjhatthana Sutra* of Buddhism reminds us: "My deeds are my closest companions. I am the beneficiary of my deeds."[12]

While reflecting on the third question in the Naikan inventory, we sometimes come face-to-face with a difficulty we have caused—even when admitting that we are wrong doesn't fit with our self-image. We might react with defensiveness: *I'm not at fault. I'm a really good person, and I didn't mean anything by what I said. That's not me.* Surprise! The unrecovered alcoholic mind blames others for our suffering. We can be sober and still hold on to our old, defended personality. Admitting when we are wrong may go against the very grain of our addictive nature, the essence of which is to escape looking at ourselves and feeling our feelings. Even in codepen-dency, compulsively focusing on another person keeps us out of touch with ourselves.

The founders of the Twelve Step program recognized this tendency and remind us of the reason for taking inventory: "For the wise have always known that no one can make much of his life until self-searching becomes a regular habit, until he is able to admit and accept what he finds, and until he patiently and persistently tries to correct what is wrong."[13] No matter how we've caused harm by what we've done or failed to do, Step Ten tells us to take responsibility and promptly admit our failing. Regardless of how other people act and how they treat us, we are responsible for our actions and reactions.

Sometimes admitting when we are wrong is a discipline in restraint. For example, adult children of alcoholic or addictive families may *always* feel wrong. A distorted sense of shame and responsibility is often at the root of our identity and present in our very being. Many of our thoughts consist of neurotic worries. In this case, taking responsibility means *not* to blame ourselves for someone else's bad mood or bad behavior. In this Step, we learn to admit only when we are wrong.

During a recent summer meditation intensive at Mind Roads Meditation Center, we did a series of guided loving kindness meditations on ourselves as children, starting with babyhood through to life as an adult. We meditated on the causes and conditions—the shaping influences—of our life. First, we looked at the people and situations that affected us as an infant, then as a five-year-old, and on through our lifespan—as a teenager and a young adult, moving up to the present. We breathed loving kindness toward our younger selves (a practice called *Tonglen);* this included sending kindness to the false self-concepts, emotional hurts, or resentments that we carry from those experiences.

As I traveled through the different periods of my life, I noticed that I'd felt fat since I was child of about ten or twelve. I hold an image of myself as chubby and uncoordinated. But, in fact, I was never all that chubby. When I weighed fifteen pounds less than now, I still felt chubby. It dawned on me that when I was young, I was actually pretty skinny. But it didn't matter how many pounds I weighed, I always felt not right. It's the affliction of the adult child of an alcoholic family. It doesn't matter what the reality is: thin, fat, healthy, sick, rich, or low in funds. We feel perpetually deficient.

Mindfulness practice and self-reflection helps us to see when we are off balance, taking too much responsibility or not enough. We can stand upon the ground of our deeds.

Mindfulness Practice for Step Ten: Taking a Naikan Inventory

Taking a Step Ten inventory by asking the Naikan questions trains us to make a habit of reflecting on our thoughts, words, and actions. This is something that both Buddhist teachings and the Twelve Steps suggest. We might even want to do a written Naikan reflection once a week or once a month, as it enriches our recovery and deepens the neural pathways that gratitude forms in our brain. Once we are aware of how our recovery is supported in concrete ways by the Universe and describe them in our Naikan writings, we can be filled with gratitude and awe.

We can do a Naikan inventory that focuses on any aspect of our life, including

- the past twenty-four hours

- a relationship with a spouse or partner

- a conflicted relationship with a co-worker

- relationships with our parents

For ideas on how to structure your Naikan reflection, read the following transcript from a Naikan inventory we did in one of our Twelve Steps and Mindfulness meetings. We framed the three questions around what supported or undermined our recovery in the past twenty-four hours. Take a seat and join in our reflections. Notice the references to the ringing of the mindfulness bell, which serves as a gentle reminder to break out of our mental reverie. You can use your own timer or a meditation bell to get a kinesthetic sense of the pace of our meeting.

(The mindfulness bell sounds.)

When you hear the mindfulness bell, let yourself ponder the first Naikan question: *What have I received in the last twenty-four hours that supported my recovery?* Spend the next ten minutes writing your reflections, letting your mind free-flow without too much thought. Remember to be very concrete and specific with your examples.

(At the end of ten minutes, the bell sounds.)

Before moving to the next question, pause and notice: What are you aware of now that you weren't aware of before? What body sensations or feelings are you experiencing right now? What was it like for you to contemplate this question? Make note of what you discover without judging or evaluating it as "good" or "bad."

Next, reflect on the second Naikan question: *What have I given to help myself and others with their sobriety in the last twenty-four hours?*

(The bell sounds.)

As you hear the bell, begin to reflect on this question. Again, spend the next ten minutes writing your reflections in a free-flowing way. Use concrete and specific examples.

(The bell sounds at the end of ten minutes.)

Pause again and notice: What are you feeling now? What are you aware of now that you weren't aware of before? What do you notice about the balance between what you receive and what you give? Are you overgiving? Undergiving? Underappreciating? Simply make note of what you discover, releasing any judgment or evaluation.

Now, move on to the third Naikan question: *What difficulties have I caused for myself or others in the last twenty-four hours, either intentionally or unintentionally?*

(The mindfulness bell sounds.)

Let the ringing of the mindfulness bell bring you deeply into this question. Spend the next ten minutes in freewriting about your reflections. Remember to be concrete and specific with your examples.

(The bell sounds again.)

As you conclude the meditation, take another moment to pause and notice: How are you feeling now? What are you aware of now that you weren't aware of before? What might you want to do differently going forward? Is there a time you realize you have been wrong? What amends are in order? Is there something you need to admit, repair with another person? Make note of what you discover, without judging or evaluating yourself.

❖ ❖ ❖

10

Making Conscious Contact

Step Eleven	We sought through prayer and meditation to improve our conscious contact with God *as we understood [God]*, praying only for knowledge of [God's] will for us and the power to carry that out.

IN STEP ELEVEN, we find that making conscious contact with Great Reality deep down within us provides a quiet peace, quenching, at last, our restless yearnings. A practice of prayer and meditation quickly becomes something we would "no more do without . . . than we would refuse air, food, or sunshine."[1]

But what are we supposed to do during these times of prayer and meditation? The founders of the Twelve Step program tell us to "ask simply that throughout the day God place in us the best understanding of [God's] will that we can have for that day, and that we be given the grace by which we may carry it out."[2]

DURING MY YEAR AT NADA MONASTERY, I MET WEEKLY WITH FATHER MICHAEL WINTERER, my spiritual director. These one-on-one meetings, and Sundays during the community volleyball game, were the only times talking was permitted. The rest of the hours of the day we kept silence, using hand signals when communication was absolutely necessary.

Meetings with Father Michael were often the highlight of my week. He lived in one of the biggest buildings on the grounds, called Saint John of the Cross Hermitage. (Some aspects of Catholicism are omnipresent.) It had two small rooms instead of one, a loft for sleeping, and a door on the bathroom. Everything was bare inside, nothing but a giant wooden crucifix hanging on the wall. Nature could be seen through the untreated windows, an expansive terrain of red dusty desert dirt, jade juniper bushes, and prickly cacti of every shape and size. That spring desert roses bloomed yellow, pink, and orange, covering the ground like a glorious Persian carpet.

Father Michael himself was a funny-looking guy, a walking anomaly. A skinny cowboy from Utah, he usually wore baggy, faded blue jeans, a white T-shirt under a gray plaid shirt, and a beat-up black-rimmed hat. He sported a scraggly red beard and mustache and thick wire-rimmed glasses that belonged on the nose of a college professor. He always seemed to be carrying books. Only when he donned his priest stole did he look like a cleric, a misfit at that.

Father Michael was funny, kind, humble, and wise. Working alongside the rest of us like a hired ranch hand, he acted as a true servant-leader. I respected him greatly. When I was twenty-four, Father Michael was one of the few kindhearted men I had ever known. I had lingering doubts about having a cowboy for a spiritual adviser. But when he spoke, they ceased. Father Michael was a learned contemplative teacher, with fifty years of study and practice under his belt. He listened with intense, twinkling eyes, leaning forward, not missing a word.

I was approaching the end of my time in the monastery, debating whether to stay longer and wondering if I should apply to become a novice with the Nada community. I wasn't sure about joining up, particularly ambivalent about the vow of celibacy. It sounded pretty grim. Then again, I was happier at Nada than I had ever been, despite the difficulties of a life of silence without TV or movies.

I sat in the worn, red stuffed chair. Across from me, Father Michael was in a roughly hewn, creaky wooden rocker. As usual, we met at eleven o'clock on a Friday morning. He listened as I presented my dilemma, tugging at his beard in thought, rocking ever so slightly in the chair.

"I've been thinking about whether to stay or not to stay at Nada," I said. "I want to stay; I like the routine and quietude. But I want to leave too.

Having relationships with people is the hard part, for me, about being out in the world. But I'd like to find a partner, maybe get married and belong in a family. I don't know what to do. How do I know what God's will is for me?"

He sat for a few moments, pondering the question. He wasn't going to give a rote answer. He cleared his throat and said, "I think God speaks to us through the deepest desires of our heart. We have to be still enough to hear which desires are true and which ones are just passing through. True desires are the breath of the Holy Spirit, speaking to you and moving you. Hold your question in meditation, listen to your heart of hearts, and wait. That's how you discern God's will. It's the quiet voice beneath the noise of your mind, that 'present moment' space between your thoughts about the past or the future."

To me, his words echoed the idea from the Twelve Steps of making "conscious contact" with the Great Reality within. If we don't have a way to calm the mind, it's nearly impossible to hear the quiet, still whispers of our heart of hearts.

I sat with my dilemma, not thinking so hard. Just breathing, noticing the cacophony of my mind. Listening for my heart to stir, nudged by the Great Reality of buddha-mind.[3] Two months later, I decided to leave Nada and rejoin the world. Still not sure it was "God's will" for me, I just did the best I could at the time. Now I realize it was a wonderful choice.

Breathing into Prayer and Meditation

Father Michael illuminated the meaning of a passage from *Twelve Steps and Twelve Traditions:* "Prayer and meditation are our principal means of conscious contact with God."[4] Mindfulness fosters our ability to listen to our heart of hearts, to be in the moment with what's true. We begin to notice the difference in quality and tone between the voice of our neurosis and that of our deepest longings.

Shunryu Suzuki-roshi, in his book *Not Always So: Practicing the True Spirit of Zen,* says this about meditation:

> So for a period of time each day, try to sit in [meditation]
> without moving, without expecting anything, as if you were in
> your last moment. Moment after moment you feel your last

instant. In each inhalation and each exhalation there are countless instants of time. Your intention is to live in each instant. First practice smoothly exhaling, then inhaling. Calmness of mind is beyond the end of your exhalation.[5]

✥ ✥ ✥

A calm mind helps us make conscious contact with our buddha nature. The instruction to "practice smoothly exhaling, then inhaling" sounds so simple that I have at times thought, *Okay, okay, I've got it. Let's move on. When are we going to get to the real spiritual stuff? There must be something more sophisticated, more advanced.* Yet Suzuki-roshi's directive is exquisitely simple: Concentrate on the out-breath, exhaling smoothly, and follow it all the way to the end. That is the way to find calmness. If we have exhaled completely, the inhale is effortless. In that momentary space between the out-breath and the in-breath, the nano-instant between thoughts, we can touch our true nature. At the end of the out-breath, we don't do anything except let ourselves be filled. Suzuki-roshi says, "If you exhale smoothly, without even trying to exhale, you are entering into the complete perfect calmness of your mind."[6]

Similarly, the founders of the Twelve Step program describe the non-striving attitude present in meditation: "As though lying upon a sunlit beach, let us relax and breathe deeply of the spiritual atmosphere with which the grace . . . surrounds us."[7]

Going against the Grain of Unmindful Living

Even if we delight in discovering this striking similarity in the Buddhist and Twelve Step traditions, we might find that breathing smoothly and completely in an easy and relaxed way goes against the grain of how we usually live. We are typically rushing around, trying to make something happen, wanting things to be different than they are.

Buddha himself warned his friends that his teachings went against the mainstream. After his awakening, Buddha's friends saw that he had visibly changed. He exuded a new serenity and lightness of being, and they "wanted what he had." But Buddha wasn't so sure. He hesitated to tell them about his enlightenment experience and subsequent insights about the path to happiness.

Legend has it that Gautama Buddha didn't think people would take him seriously. He shooed his friends away. They came back. He sent them away again, and they still came back. It's said that the great god Brahma interceded, imploring Buddha to expound his teachings, and only then did he reluctantly agree. Buddha said:

> Dear Friends,
>
> This Dharma which I have realized is indeed profound,
> difficult to perceive, difficult to comprehend, tranquil, exalted,
> not within the sphere of logic, subtle, and is to be understood
> by the wise . . . This Dharma . . . goes against the stream,
> which is abstruse, profound, difficult to perceive and subtle.[8]

❖ ❖ ❖

All these centuries later, we can use exactly the same words to describe the Buddha's teachings. To understand them, we must listen with the heart, let the body and mind drop away, and contemplate the teachings for weeks, months, even years.

Watering the Seeds of Our Buddha Nature

Buddha taught that within us all—within me, within you—lives the potential of an enlightened being. We each have the seeds of a buddha nature, a spiritual essence. *Buddha seeds* is a famous term in Buddhism, perhaps like *Son of God* in Christianity. Each of us, every being, has buddha seeds within. The Buddha goes so far as to say that even beings in hell have the seeds of awakening within. Thích Nhất Hanh says, "If you want to be a Buddha ask, if not me, who else?"

When I hear these ideas, one of my first responses is that I really want to believe that I have buddha seeds within me. But in my addictive ways, I have always been looking for happiness outside myself. That part of me immediately thinks, *Yeah, yeah, yeah. That might be true for other people, but not for me. I don't know about those buddha-seed-things. I know about loneliness, craving, and anger. No beauty-nature-wondrous-mystery-being for this girl. I'm just scared of being bad and feeling bad.*

Saying that we have buddha seeds within us does not mean that they're realized or that we're even conscious of them yet. Yet the seeds are always there. Always have been. Always will be. According to fourteenth-century Zen master Bassui:

> From the beginning everyone is complete and perfect . . .
> The movement of a newborn baby's legs and arms is . . . the
> splendid work of its original nature. The bird flying, the hare
> running, the sun rising, the moon sinking, the wind blowing,
> the clouds moving, all things that shift and change are due to . . .
> [the splendor of] their own original nature.[9]

❖ ❖ ❖

We can cultivate the goodness and beauty part of our nature through the prayer and meditation advised in Step Eleven. We water the seeds of our buddha nature so they can bloom.

Living from a Full Cup

Ten years after leaving Nada monastery, I drained my savings to take a sojourn to India. I went with a group of twelve Americans to study meditation, see the sights, and visit Mother Teresa's mission.

THE STREETS OF CALCUTTA stunk with rotting garbage, sweating bodies, and stale urine. At the first rays of morning light, sidewalks transformed into impromptu kitchens, smoldering with charcoal-burning cook fires. Street people came from every direction out of nowhere, now cooking *pooris*, curried peas, and cardamom-scented *masala* chai tea.

Thirty minutes post–morning shower, I discovered that a fine coat of dusty grit was beginning to clog the pores of my skin. At 9:00 a.m. it was already steamy hot. The windows of our taxi were rolled open, wafting waves of stench. Crawling through traffic, we passed rangy camels defecating in the streets and oxen-pulled carts next to shiny white Mercedes-Benz taxis. Rickshaws wove in and out of what might have been a lane of vehicles. Glimpsing a white woman from the West, beggars reached through the lowered windows to tug at my clothes, mothers with smudged faces, bony babies laid swaddled in their arms. Lepers wrapped in rags and maimed children stared with empty eyes from the street. Hawkers selling their wares trailed the cars, with angry drivers shouting, honking, and cursing.

The chaos in the streets was fascinating, overwhelming, and disturbing to me. How do people deal with all this hardship? How do they survive the poverty? What can I do to help these children? Will anything help? In India, the suffering showed. It was visible. The kind of suffering I had known was more hidden, less life threatening. But I thought I recognized the look of hurt and fear, sensed the desperation.

We inched along the streets for over an hour, finally reaching the adobe-walled compound. A remarkably ordinary wooden door stood beneath a modest blue sign with stenciled white letters: "Missionaries of Charity, Motherhouse, Kolcata." Three homeless, crippled men sat on the steps, hands outstretched.

Once we were inside the door, all chaos ceased. A blessed quiet enveloped us, a small respite from the heartache and din. The smell of bleach, strong enough to tickle the hairs of my nose, filled the air. The atrium held tidy rows of angel-wing begonias; white jasmine and yellow daylilies lined the stone walkways. Vines climbed the walled compound, purple clematis framed a tiny niche with a statue of the Virgin Mary, water lilies floated in the standing fountain. Nuns in white saris bordered in blue padded by, looking like they had important work to do: saving souls and lifting dying people off the sidewalks, helping them to die with dignity.

Much to our surprise and delight, Mother Teresa was in residence. Our guide announced she would see us momentarily. "Would your group like to wait in the chapel? Mother will be in to see you shortly. Please take a few moments to visit with Our Lord."

Our group leader said, "Yes, Sister, we'll be happy to wait."

The chapel was immaculate, smelling of incense, candle wax, and the lingering scent of cleaning solution. A simple wooden altar stood in the center of a bare room, tall ivory tapers held by curly brass candleholders at each end, framing a miniature Jesus on the cross. Pope John Paul II looked down from the single, enormous portrait on the wall. Cushions were stacked in the corner to sit on, and there were small benches for kneeling in prayer. Fans hugged the ceiling, whirling their arms in circles, swishing hot air. I sat on the floor, leaning against the coolness of the white wall.

It was as quiet as soft velvet in the chapel. You could almost touch the peacefulness, as if it were alive, breathing there in the room. I settled into the silence, wrapping it around my body like a luscious coat. It was then that I noticed the far wall had a bank of transom windows, open to the street below. Here, in the midst of the mayhem and stench of the streets of Calcutta, was an oasis of calm. It struck me that the chapel itself was a metaphor. Peace can be found in the midst of the ups and downs and chaos of our lives. Not elsewhere. Meditation gives access to an oasis of calm right in the middle of the muddle.

Mother Teresa entered, small and bent, skin weathered with age, and face radiant with inner joy. As I stood to bow in greeting, the top of her veiled head barely reached my shoulder. (Even though I had seen pictures of her, I somehow thought she would be a giant in a white dress.) She went around the group, made contact with each of us, patted my arm, and made a sign of the cross over my head as a blessing.

"Sit down, my children. You should be comfortable. Why are you here?"

A member of our group said, "We're here studying Bhakti yoga and meditation, visiting holy sites in India. We wanted to see your mission and lend our support to your work."

"That's good. God loves all of us, his children, but especially the least among us. God asks us to help his dear ones, the poorest of the poor. I hope that when you return to your country, you will be moved to do that."

Mother Teresa told us about hearing God's call while riding the train in what was then Yugoslavia, "the whisper of intuition" that led her to India. She talked about the rigor of the schedule followed by the Missionaries of

Charity—their practice of prayer and meditation each morning before leaving to work in the streets and again upon returning, before evening supper. She said daily prayer and meditation helped to keep the nuns from getting disheartened by the great suffering all around them.

"You should pray and meditate every day, so you know that you are loved, so you feel the presence of God's love in your life. This is the only way you can truly help others and serve the poorest of the poor. We have to give from a full heart, one that is saturated with love, overflowing to others. Before we can give freely, we have to know that we are loved. This is why you should pray and meditate every day. So you can remember you are loved, letting it fill your heart and your body. Let it fill every cell of your being. Then give it all away." She smiled. "Do you see?"

We bobbed our heads. No words came.

Mother Teresa stayed a while longer, visiting with each of us, asking where we were from in the United States and what we did for a living. A small bundle of intensity and drive, she made fierce eye contact.

I had a money belt tied around my waist, under a billowy green peasant skirt. I unzipped it and pulled out a large wad of bills. That year, I'd approached all my friends, asking them if they wanted to make a donation to the Missionaries of Charity for their holiday giving. I had collected a nice sum and promised to hand carry the money to Calcutta. I didn't know I would be placing the gift directly into Mother Teresa's hands.

"Mother, this is a gift from my friends and family in Saint Paul, Minnesota."

She tucked it under her white sari, face crinkled into a broad smile.

"God bless you, child."

She folded my hand in hers, touching them to her heart. Not a word spoken.

Then she shifted weight. In a flash, glint in her eye, Mother Teresa asked, "Say, would you like one of my business cards?"

I nodded, tongue-tied.

She pulled a pale blue card out of her mysteriously pocketed sari, handing it to me.

In another instant, she was encircled by an entourage of sisters in blue-bordered saris, swooped away down the narrow hall, needed for pressing mission work.

I looked down, turning the card over in my hand. It read:

GOD, GRANT ME THE SERENITY TO ACCEPT
THE THINGS I CANNOT CHANGE,

THE COURAGE TO CHANGE THE THINGS I CAN,

AND THE WISDOM TO KNOW THE DIFFERENCE.

Missionaries of Charity

❖ ❖ ❖

I carry that moment with me still. Caretaking for others was my way of life. I was the adult child of an alcoholic family, a professional psychotherapist, a stepmother and grandmother, and an eldercare provider for my aging mother. Too many times, I gave at the expense of myself.

Mother Teresa's message was that giving should flow from a *full* cup, inspired by the energy of prayer and meditation, arising from the experience of being loved just as we are at this moment, without exception. The Missionaries of Charity themselves spend two hours each morning in liturgy and meditation. Before going out to serve the poorest of the poor, they steep in conscious contact with a Power greater than themselves. Fill up their hearts. In the evening when they return from working in the orphanages or in the streets, they spend another one to two hours in prayer and meditation. Refilling their hearts. They meditate before they eat.

Oh, I see. That's how they do it.

That's how they can stand the unbearable suffering all around them. They spend time every day watering their buddha seeds with grace. That's how they can give with such joy and generosity. I want to meditate with that kind of consistency and dedication.

No Striving—Just Sit

In my early years of working Step Eleven, all that seeking through prayer and meditation seemed like a lot of effort. I realize now that I was striving, applying my usual style of managing and controlling to my spiritual practice, working and waiting for something to happen. And if it didn't, I thought I must be doing something wrong. Now, thirty-some years later, I think that conscious contact simply takes time on the cushion. No matter if the experience is restful or frustrating. Just sit, and see what happens.

COLIN WAS A THIRTYSOMETHING HIGH SCHOOL TEACHER in one of our Fundamentals of Meditation classes at Mind Roads Meditation Center. At the beginning of the class, he asked a million questions. He furrowed his forehead while he thought. Colin had read many books on meditation and knew a great deal about the theories and practices of Buddhism. He often asked if there was a book on this subject or that topic related to what we were covering in class. But he didn't have time to do any sitting meditation.

I finally said to him, "Stop reading! Take the time you usually spend reading about meditation and do sitting meditation instead. For the weeks you are in this class, don't read anymore. Just sit meditation. Then see what happens."

To his credit, he did exactly that. He took the suggestion to heart and started sitting meditation every morning.

At the end of eight weeks, which isn't very long, he looked like a different man—not so tightly wound, the furrow in his brow less pronounced. He had dropped into his heart, and it was starting to open.

Colin's wife, who was also in the class, said, "He's nicer."

I replied, "My husband says that about me too."

IN THE TWELVE STEPS AND TWELVE TRADITIONS, it says: "There is a direct linkage among self-examination, meditation, and prayer. Taken separately, these practices can bring much belief and benefit. But when they are logically related and interwoven, the result is an unshakeable foundation for life."[10]

But we can't think our way there. We can't strive our way there. We need to just sit, mindful of the moment.

Conscious Contact Lets Our True Self Emerge

Thích Nhất Hạnh, referring to Buddhist scripture called The Lotus Sutra, talks about how to make conscious contact with our true self. He describes an old monastic practice in which monks carved a cave from rock to live in. They didn't build huts out of wood and stone. Rather, they employed the same process a sculptor uses to create a statue, carving away stone to make a shape.

While on a pilgrimage to China a few years ago, I was amazed to see the intricate work of these ancient monks. How long it must have taken to carve a home out of a solid, unrelenting rock, the enormous patience and determination required to persevere.

In meditation, like the sculptor, we "take away the rock to let the shape emerge."[11] We don't bring in enlightenment from the outside. We remove the confusion. We remove the ignorance. We remove the lack of forgiveness. We unveil the delusions of Mara, letting go of beliefs that we are incapable of bearing painful feelings, that we need the pleasures of drugs or alcohol or food or sex to relieve our distress, or that we can be spared from loss and death.

Buddhism teaches that we are in a state of ignorance if we think we are unworthy, inherently defective, needing a lover, teacher, or another person to fill us up. That's why we may chase unhealthy, codependent relationships with other people, believing they can somehow give us the part we lack, the part that will make us whole. In such situations, Buddhism says, we have forgotten our buddha nature. Once we remove these confusions, enlightenment reveals itself.

Buddhists say that we are never separated from this nature of awakening, even when we feel the most stuck. With prayer and meditation, we remember our true face, our original nature. Our true buddha nature is described as the capacity to be beautiful, good, and true. It is something within and between, rather than outside us. Thích Nhất Hanh says:

> In the beginning we imagine that buddha [or God as we understand God] is an entity that exists outside of us . . . We imagine that buddha is someone out there, but that is not a deep practice. An [ancient teacher] said that you have to take refuge in the buddha in yourself, so he advised us to recite, "Taking refuge in the buddha in myself."[12]

❖ ❖ ❖

Mindfulness Practice for Step Eleven

In the spirit of "different strokes for different folks," learn a variety of ways to meditate. Changing life circumstances sometimes require that we vary our approach. Following is an overview of four core meditation techniques you can try.[13] Experiment to find personal ways of deepening your conscious contact with the Great Reality within. Work with one practice in particular for a while until it begins to work with you.

"Non-Meditating"—Resting the Mind

Buddha said the basic, true nature of the mind can be directly experienced by allowing the mind to just rest. In *The Joy of Living,* Yongey Mingyur Rinpoche echoes this instruction, suggesting that we think of sitting still and resting the mind as an exercise in "non-meditating." This exercise is a very old Buddhist practice designed to "take the pressure off thinking you have to achieve some goal or experience some special state."[14]

What do we do on the cushion? We simply pay attention and become curious about whatever is happening within ourselves, letting go of judging it.

I often hear people say things such as, "I had a really good meditation session." Or "I had a really bad meditation session. My monkey mind was all over the place and I couldn't make my mind be quiet. I wasn't at all peaceful."

I challenge them: "What is a 'really good' meditation session?" I ask because I want to make people conscious of their expectations. Actually, there is no such thing as a good or bad meditation session. Whatever happens in our meditation is the experience of those moments. It is neither good nor bad. It just is.

When meditating, we are not trying to make ourselves be a certain way. We don't make ourselves do anything except sit down on the cushion, hold the posture, and breathe. Once seated, we are simply present to and curious about whatever arises, observing our mind as we would watch clouds pass in the sky. *Oh, look at that, a dark little self-pity cloud just went through. Oh, look at that, a poofy grateful cloud went through.* We just notice what is, with the bare attention of openness and curiosity. We acknowledge, with kindness, whatever is happening.

The following "experiment" is much like the breath awareness practice introduced in chapter 1. At the same time, it is shorter, less formal, with any pressure to "do good" at meditating (hopefully) removed.

The idea is to simply rest the mind for three minutes by trying this:

> *Sit with your spine straight.* Make sure you can breathe easily, with the body relaxed.
>
> *Allow your mind to rest.* Let it go anywhere it goes. Whatever happens—or doesn't happen—is part of the "mental experiment." Simply notice it. You might feel physically comfortable or uncomfortable. You might hear sounds or smell smells in your environment. You might get lost in thoughts or become aware of feelings of anger, sadness, fear, or other emotions. Just go with any of it. As Yongey Mingyur Rinpoche reminds us, "Anything that happens—or doesn't happen—is simply part of the experience of allowing your mind to rest."[15] Don't try to meditate.
>
> *When the three minutes are up, reflect.* Ask yourself: How was that experiment? Don't judge or evaluate or try to explain. Just review what happened and how you felt.
>
> Congratulations! You have just meditated for three minutes.

❖ ❖ ❖

The only difference between meditation and the everyday process of sensing, thinking, and feeling is holding a mindset of "bare awareness" toward whatever is happening. We learn to observe ourselves without criticism or judgment, with openness and curiosity.

You can build on the practice of resting the mind by beginning to sit in formal meditation, using the breath awareness practices introduced in chapter 1.

Object Meditation

Some beginning meditators fight the sounds, sights, smells, or other sensations that they experience while meditating, thinking of these internal events as unwelcome distractions. Instead, you can make them the object of your attention. Buddhism refers to this technique as "'self-antidote,' using the source of distraction itself as a means of freedom from distraction."[16]

The idea behind this practice is to focus on an object for five minutes. Try this:

> *Sit with a straight spine.* Relax your body. Let your mind rest, just as it is, for a few moments.
>
> *Deliberately rest your awareness on a specific object.* These can include the following:
>
> - Physical sensations. Be curious about what you feel in your body, such as a tingling in your leg, or tune into the sensations in a specific area, such as your hands, jaw, or forehead.
> - Painful sensations. Rather than fight physical pain, trying to push it away, become interested in it instead. Notice the sensations of a headache or toothache. Observe the experience of being cold, hot, hungry, or tired. See how the sensations change as you become aware of them.
> - Forms. Focus on the sensory perceptions of seeing. Really *look* at the flame of a candle, the variations of blue in the sky, the shades of scarlet in the autumn leaves, or the tones of green in new grass.
> - Sounds. Tune in to what you hear in the environment, such as the ring of a cell phone, the whoosh of cars going by, or the beautiful sound of a bird call.
> - Smells. Take in the smells in your environment, such as the scent of incense or the aromas of cooking food. Make them the focus of your meditation.
> - Tastes. Eat mindfully, noticing the taste sensations of your food and paying attention to when you are hungry, when you are full.

Be aware of your object of choice for a few moments. Just notice it. Bring your awareness to what you experience moment by moment while you are looking, smelling, hearing, feeling, or tasting the object of your meditation.

Let go of your concentration. Just let the mind rest for a few more moments.

Reflect on the experience. Ask yourself: How was that experiment?

❖ ❖ ❖

Movement Meditation

In this form of meditation, we concentrate on the sensations of the body in motion. This is the basis of walking meditation and a mindful yoga practice.

In our everyday life, we rarely move or stretch simply for the experience of it. An alternative is to move with no particular aim and without trying to get anywhere. In Buddhist meditation, this is called *apranibita,* meaning "aimlessness." Each movement is taken slowly and deliberately. Each step is enjoyed.

Walking meditation is an ideal way to begin this practice. Try this:

Walk in slow motion for ten minutes. You can do this inside your home or outside in an open area.

As you move, focus on the sensations of your legs in motion. Experience your weight shifting. Observe the feel of the sole of your foot making contact with the ground, your muscles contracting and releasing. Notice each part of the experience:

- Stand upright and still, allowing your arms to hang comfortably by your sides or be clasped behind your back.

- Keep your eyes downcast enough to avoid distractions and to see where you are going.

- Notice the intention to raise one foot and place your attention on that foot.
- Raise the foot a little and momentarily hold it there.
- Notice the intention to move the foot forward.
- Move the foot forward and hold it for a moment just above the ground.
- Notice the intention to place the foot on the ground.
- Place the foot on the ground.
- Repeat the process with the other foot, letting go of trying to control your breathing or your walking.

❖ ❖ ❖

Remember to observe each part of the experience. As you move, experience your weight shifting. Notice the feel of the sole of your foot making contact with the ground and your muscles contracting and releasing throughout each step.

Mentally Reciting a Phrase

In this practice, we turn a phrase in our mind, adding it to the cycle of breathing in and breathing out, like a mantra. We used this technique in the Three Refuges Prayer in chapter 3 and again for the loving kindness meditation in chapter 5.

When we get caught in the "stinking thinking" of addiction, compulsions, or codependency, this technique can be a great consolation. Mental recitation gives us something else to do with our mind in those moments, redirecting our neural impulses to a new track of thought.

In keeping with any faith tradition, a wide variety of phrases can be used as a focus in a concentration meditation. For example, in *Alcoholics Anonymous,* it is suggested that we use the Prayer of Saint Francis—always a most beautiful choice. A familiar portion of that prayer is as follows:

LORD, MAKE ME A CHANNEL
OF THY PEACE—

THAT WHERE THERE IS HATRED,
I MAY BRING LOVE—

THAT WHERE THERE IS WRONG, I MAY BRING
THE SPIRIT OF FORGIVENESS—

THAT WHERE THERE IS DISCORD,
I MAY BRING HARMONY—

❖ ❖ ❖

Other phrases or prayers can be used, such as a verse from a psalm, a line from a poem, a stanza from the Bible or other holy text, or the Serenity Prayer. Many times, when my mind is agitated, brewing a storm, I like to use something short and sweet.

What's happening as we use mental recitation is that we're getting out of our own way when we meditate. Not doing anything. Not making ourselves relax. Just letting ourselves breathe and thinking, "Let the buddha-in-me breathe. Let the buddha-in-me walk."[17] And while the buddha-in-us is breathing, we can just kick back and enjoy the sensations of breathing. That's all. We are there in the moment, noticing and enjoying what it's like to breathe. Then, while the buddha-in-me is breathing, I *am* the breath—me with all others breathing at that moment. *One.*

Try any of these:

Recite a mantra-like phrase silently in your mind as you breathe.
For example: "Let the buddha-in-me breathe *in,* let the buddha-in-me breathe *out.* Or "Breathing in, I know I am breathing *in.* Breathing out, I know I am breathing *out.*"

Add a mantra-like phrase to your walking or movement meditation. You could simply recite, "Let the buddha-in-me walk."

Combine breath awareness with loving kindness meditation. Recite a loving kindness blessing in your mind with each breath, such as, "May I be peaceful" on the in-breath, "and happy" on the out-breath. Pair one blessing with each full breath.

Combine loving kindness blessings with walking meditation.
As you lift your foot to take a step, say, "May I have ease of
well-being." As you place your foot on the ground, say, "in this
life." Again, recite one blessing with each step.

❖ ❖ ❖

With that same intimate awareness, we can recognize our life as we live
it. There are the sensations of showering in this warm water. There is the
experience of reading this story to my grandchild. There is feeling my husband's breath on my skin as I lie next to him sleeping here, and I can let
myself be fully present to our moments of lovemaking. We know firsthand
what it is like to be here in this precious life.

11

Remembering Our True Face

Step Twelve

Having had a spiritual awakening as the result of these steps, we tried to carry this message to alcoholics, and to practice these principles in all our affairs.

THE FIRST PHRASE IN STEP TWELVE mentions *spiritual awakening* and describes it as the result of working all the previous Steps. Since the beginning of the Twelve Step fellowship, members have grappled with this term. It is central to recovery and yet resists all our attempts at definition.

How does the Buddhist literature describe a *spiritual awakening*? I went to a text called the *Dhammapada*, meaning "the words of Buddha." (I suppose it could be called the "Big Book" of Buddhism.) Here are the words Buddha used to describe awakening, in an ancient verse titled "Crossing the Stream":

> Few cross over the river. Most are stranded on this side. On the riverbank they run up and down. But the wise person, following the way, crosses over, crosses over beyond the reach of death. Free from desire, free from possessions, free from attachment and appetite, following the seven lights of awakening, and rejoicing greatly in one's freedom, in this world the wise person becomes oneself a light, pure, shining, free.[1]

163

Despite the freedom and joy that come with awakening, Buddha recognizes that not many people choose a spiritual path. They run up and down the riverbank, he says, stranded on the shore of attachment and appetite.

While I was using drugs, tied in emotional knots from life in my alcoholic family, I certainly felt like I was running, chasing my tail. Seeking belonging and relief from loneliness in all the wrong places. Looking for peace of mind outside myself, trying to escape and "get the hell out of here" from life. Stranded and alone.

The wise person, on the other hand, "crosses over beyond the reach of death." For those of us in the Twelve Step program, "death" is our disease: the addiction, compulsion, or codependency that ravages our soul. For some of us, the risk of our addictive ways and the prison of our addictive mind involve the possibility of real, physical death. "If we cannot stop, the course of our destruction will just continue."[2]

Through the Twelve Step program, we cross over to a new way of living. We awaken to freedom from cravings, shallow desires, and clinging to what we cannot change. We are promised that we can become "free from desire, free from possessions, free from attachment and appetite."[3] Free from our addictive mind. If we follow the Twelve Steps—the lights of awakening—we can, ourselves, become pure, illuminating the way for others to come. We can live the way of kindness in the world, in "all of our affairs," and let our true face shine.

Awakening the Mind of Love

What is actually happening here, in this hard-to-understand business of a spiritual awakening? Buddhists say that awakening is the rising of *bodhichitta* energy, called the "mind of love." This energy is "the motivating force for the practice of mindful living," inspiring "a deep wish . . . to bring happiness to others."[4] When bodhichitta is aroused, we desire to practice the Twelve Step principles in all the affairs of our daily life, reaching out to others who are suffering. In Buddhism, this is called the "Great Aspiration."

The first part of the word bodhichitta, *bodhi*, means "awake" or, in another translation, "enlightened." In yet another translation, "openhearted." The second syllable is *chitta*, meaning "mind-heart or attitude."

In the Eastern view, mind and heart are not split, hence the phrase *mind-heart.*

Bodhichitta energy changes our attitude. We don't want to be hardened and defensive anymore. We don't want to be separate and alone anymore. We don't want to be pretentious or dishonest with others. We want our heart to open. Buddhists say bodhichitta is the only energy that really heals, reportedly able to transform even the hardest and crustiest of hearts, the most prejudiced and fearful of minds.

Arising bodhichitta opens the "soft spot in our heart."⁵ The soft spot is the part of us that is touched by the kindness of another. It recognizes beauty in the trees and the flowers, the blue of the sky, and music so beautiful that it makes you cry. But this very same soft spot feels fear, loneliness, and confusion. *That* soft spot.

Most addicts—dare I say—have worked very hard to protect that soft spot from getting hurt (again). In recovery, we start to see that at the core of our compulsions is the desire to escape from feeling pain.

When I first started practicing meditation thirty-some years ago, I wanted it to help me escape from pain. I was in for a surprise.

AFTER RETURNING HOME FROM NADA MONASTERY, I participated for the next twelve months in the Extended Ignatian Retreat offered by the Cenacle House in Wayzata, Minnesota. We studied the Ignatian Exercises, meditated at home for an hour each day, and met with our spiritual director twice a month.

Then in 1980, the Sisters of the Cenacle, with the members of their order dwindling, started a program to train lay people in spiritual direction. I studied for the following nine years to become a spiritual director, attending Wednesday morning class and meeting with a small group of other spiritual direction colleagues once a month. My group stayed together far beyond the assigned time.

One afternoon we sat around the large wooden table in the library of the Cenacle House, the room scented by lemon Pledge and dusty books.

One member of our group checked in, saying, "I didn't think a spiritual practice would be like this. I thought that I would be able to rise above my problems, be more removed from them. The picture in my mind was of a stronger me, drawing from a wellspring of faith, being stoic in the face of distress. Instead, meditating and spiritual practice has made me feel more. I feel everything more. When I hurt, I hurt more. When sad, I am filled with sorrow. When I laugh, I laugh more deeply. When I'm happy, I'm overjoyed. I feel what I feel more fully. I guess that means I'm more alive!"

My colleague was describing "having had a spiritual awakening." Awakening isn't an escape, a "spiritual bypassing" of our difficulties, but rather, a profound and deep connection to life.

The energy of bodhichitta, the desire to help others, naturally arises from this open, soft spot of our heart. We don't need to try to make it happen. Our job is to allow our heart to open. Quit trying to protect it. Simply water the seeds of our buddha nature. The mind of love awakens itself, as a fruit of our practice, as a result of working these Steps.

Two Levels of Bodhichitta

Buddhist texts describe two levels of bodhichitta, *absolute* and *relative*. Absolute bodhichitta is a state of "direct insight into the nature of mind . . . where there is no distinction between self and other."[6] A person in absolute bodhichitta recognizes each living being as a "buddha-to-be," having compassion and kindness for even the most difficult person. Holy beings such as Mother Teresa, Thích Nhất Hanh, or the Dalai Lama come to mind.

For the rest of us, awakening may be a much slower road called "the gradual path of relative bodhichitta." Buddhist tradition says we can train in relative bodhichitta by two practices: aspiration and application.

The First Bodhichitta Practice: Aspiration

In this practice we hold a heartfelt desire toward a particular outcome, as we did in loving kindness practice. Here, we incline our mind toward attaining awakening in order to help all "living beings achieve . . . happiness and freedom from pain and suffering."[7] We aspire, simply "desiring to desire," to help others—those still suffering from addictions and alcoholism, family members of addicts and alcoholics, and all living beings.

To my mind, there is a dawning of aspiration bodhichitta in Step Twelve. Through a spiritual awakening that results from these Twelve

Steps, we realize that "we are not the only one." The desire to give freely and be of service bubbles up in our heart. We experience how the happiness of others is indeed our own happiness.

The Second Bodhichitta Practice: Application

This bodhichitta practice "is often compared . . . to actually taking the steps to arrive at the intended destination" of helping other beings.[8] Simply put, we do the work of giving, applying the principles of the Twelve Step program "in all our affairs." The authors of *Twelve Steps and Twelve Traditions* pose questions similar to the following to help us:

> Can we bring a spirit of love and tolerance into our relationships?
>
> Can we have faith and confidence in other people?
>
> Can we carry the Twelve Step spirit into our daily work?
>
> Can we meet our responsibilities to the world at large?
>
> Can we find the joy of living?[9]

Awakening in the Space between Thoughts

We have access to the warm-hearted openness of bodhichitta any time, any place, any moment. Each time we sit in meditation, we can touch that very buddha nature in the calmness at the end of the out-breath. Right in that tiny instant before the in-breath, there is a glimmer of our true nature, a nano-space between our thoughts. Right there, at the end of the breath, is calmness. We find it in that little, teeny space where we stop trying to do life all by ourselves, where we just let ourselves be breathed.

At that instant, we touch our inner buddha nature. This is our true face. It has been there all along. We are just remembering, like recognizing the countenance of a dear, old friend. "Your true nature is something never lost to you even in moments of delusion," says the Zen master Huang Po, "nor is it gained at the moment of Enlightenment."[10]

I am comforted, when afraid, by following the out-breath all the way to the end. Then, just waiting, I trust that the in-breath will come, allowing myself to be breathed, surrendering self-will for that instant. The mind of awakening, bodhichitta, is in the experience of this one moment, free of concepts, open to what is. Open-hearted. Open-minded. Bare.

From the wellspring of bodhichitta, the desire to help others rises. We wish to carry the message of these Steps to those still suffering. We reach out to help our fellows struggling with alcoholism, compulsions, and the effects of an addictive family upbringing. And, in mindfulness practice, our heart opens to all living beings. The mind of love within us holds all its dear ones in tenderness.

NOT TOO LONG AGO, I SAT ON THE LEAF-PRINTED FUTON on the back porch. Sage-painted walls and wide-open screen windows overlooked the back garden. As is typical in August in Minnesota, the tomato plants were bent down, laden with ripe red fruit. No chickadees splashed in the birdbath this morning, but a brown baby bunny chewed the leftover lettuce. The humming of cicadas filled the air.

I had just hung up from talking on the telephone with Eijun Linda Ruth Cutts. We try to confer once a month or so for a spiritual direction session. After greetings, she said, "It's nice to hear your voice."

Your voice is like music, comforting and strong. I am so fortunate to have such a wise and compassionate person to talk with, I thought.

My sister Anne and I had driven to Rochester, Minnesota, the day before, visiting dear Auntie Marie, my mother's last surviving sister. She is nearly ninety-four years old and failing. We wanted to say our good-byes while she was still somewhat alert. I felt sadness, touching the loss of my own mother. She and Marie sound and look a lot alike, more and more alike the longer they lived.

I wonder if my sister Anne and I will look more and more alike as we age. Will we live into our nineties too?

When Marie dies, my mother's generation will be no more.

Sadness gathered in my throat. We talked with my aunt about her childhood on the homestead in Montana, the hardships and adventure of it all. Raymond, the only boy in the family, died from intestinal blockage at the age of four because my grandparents couldn't get him to the hospital in time. The horse and wagon couldn't make the thirty miles to town in fewer than three hours. He died in my grandmother's arms along the road. The tragedy of it broke all their hearts.

Marie's daughter, my cousin Nita, had collected old photos and put them into an orange and green album titled "Memories." There was my mother with her sisters, young and vibrant. There were my grandparents, standing by their son's grave, looking stricken. There we were as little children, tiny and innocent. The photos showed the great cycle of life and death, what Buddhists call the "Great Matter," turning.

I was telling Eijun Linda Ruth how, upon returning home to my husband, Jim, I wanted to cling to him. Hold him close and not let go. He is fifteen years my senior and would soon turn seventy-two years of age. Although he is healthy and strong, still long-distance cycling with his buddies both summer and winter, I fear his aging. Now that my parents' generation is nearly gone, death and the inevitability of losing him seem far more near.

I asked, "How can I apply meditation practice here? What will help this fear?"

Linda Ruth began to talk about Thích Nhất Hanh's practice of hugging meditation. She has been doing this meditation with her children, now adults, and her husband ever since attending a workshop he held in California many years ago. I suppose we could call it mindful hugging. She said the concreteness of this practice pulls a person back to the present moment, away from ghosts of the past or fears of the future.

"Pay attention to the physical sensations of hugging. With Jim, breathe in and let the touch of his body come into your awareness. If he's willing, you could breathe together, in sync. But that's not necessary. In your mind, as you breathe in, say, 'I know you are real.' Linger with it. Be with his love for you and your love for him. Say, 'I know you are real.' Do that and see what happens." She said if we do this practice, soon we'll be so full of loving there won't be room for fear.

Her instructions reminded me of a similar practice I had read about in Thích Nhất Hanh's book *Teachings on Love*. There, he says to look at the person we love and breathe in the thought: *I know you are there for me and I am so happy.*[11] After doing that practice for a few months, I had forgotten about it until that moment. That phrase came back with the sound of Eijun Linda Ruth's voice. After finishing the call, I closed my eyes, thought of Jim, and breathed him in. He has been a wonderful life companion. I have learned kindness and love from him. *You are real.*

Thank you. You are there for me and I am so happy.

The faces of others began to float into my mind. One at a time, I breathed them in.

My sister Anne. The difficulties we've faced. The super yummy "Dolly Date" cookies she makes from Grandma's recipe. How she's always bringing presents from her trips to Japan. *You are real.*

My lovely, growing-up-so-fast granddaughters, Grace, Julia, and Olivia. Their beautiful, cherub faces. The ways the older girls have sweetly demonstrated how to text and taught us how to do things on the computer. How the littlest one has a mischievous glint in her eye. *You are real.*

My dear friends.

My spiritual teachers.

The warmth of the sun, the breeze through the window.

The light of awakening, the heart opening.

You are real.

And I am so happy.

May *all* beings, in all the ten directions, be happy.

NOTES

Epigraph

1. Shantideva, "Miracle of Awakening," in *Bodhicharyavatara (A Guide to the Bodhisattva's Way of Life)*, quoted in Jack Kornfield, ed., adapted by Eknath Easwaran, *Teachings of the Buddha* (Boston: Shambhala Publications, 2007), 132.

1. Joining the Great We

1. Wikipedia: The Free Encyclopedia, "Buddhism," http://en.wikipedia.org/wiki/Buddhism. The "Four Insights on the Reality of How Things Are," among the most fundamental Buddhist teachings, appear many times throughout the most ancient Buddhist texts, the Pali Canon.

2. A. Lutz and others, "Long-Term Meditators Self-Induce High-Amplitude Gamma Synchrony during Mental Practice," *Proceedings of the National Academy of Sciences* 101, no. 163 (2004), 69–73.

3. Buddha taught the "Eightfold Path" as the way to emancipate ourselves from suffering; this consists of the following:

Right view
Right intention
Right effort
Right action
Right speech
Right livelihood
Right mindfulness
Right meditation

4. *Dharma teacher* refers to an ordained Buddhist priest or spiritual adviser. *Dharma* is a Pali word for "the truth, the way things are," most frequently used in reference to Buddha's teachings. A dharma teacher expounds on the meaning of Buddhist texts and helps students apply them to the challenges or circumstances of their lives.

5. Thích Nhất Hạnh, *The Heart of the Buddha's Teaching* (New York: Broadway Books, 1999), 67.

Thích Nhất Hạnh is a poet, Zen master, and author of more than thirty books on Buddhism. He served as chair of the Buddhist delegation to the Paris Peace Talks during the Vietnam War, and was nominated by Dr. Martin Luther King Jr. for the Nobel Peace Prize. He is the founder of Plum Village, a meditation community in southwestern France.

6. *Twelve Steps and Twelve Traditions*, 14th printing (New York: Alcoholics Anonymous World Services, 1976), 121.

7. Yongey Mingyur Rinpoche, *The Joy of Living: Unlocking the Secret and Science of Happiness*, 1st paperback ed. (New York: Three Rivers Press, 2007), 55.

8. This is a practice suggested by Thích Nhất Hạnh.

2. Coming To

1. A "we" version of the Twelve Steps is used by the Twelve Steps and Mindfulness group meeting at the Mind Roads Meditation Center in Saint Paul, MN. This practice is in keeping with the original Six Steps of Alcoholics Anonymous written by Dr. Bob in 1938—each of which began with "We." In future versions of the Steps, this word was redacted because "it was clearly implied." Dick B., *The Akron Genesis of Alcoholics Anonymous*, rev. ed. (Kihei, HI: Paradise Research Publications, 1998), 256.

The original Six Steps read as follows:

1. We admitted we were licked, that we were powerless over alcohol.
2. We made a moral inventory of our defects or sins.
3. We confessed or shared our shortcomings with another person in confidence.
4. We made restitution to all those we had harmed by our drinking.
5. We tried to help other alcoholics, with no thought of reward in money or prestige.
6. We prayed to whatever God we thought there was for power to practice these precepts.

2. This phrase is taken from a Daily Zen Sutra in the Buddhist tradition, "Great Vows for All." The following version is recited at the Clouds in Water Zen Center in Saint Paul, MN (www.cloudsinwater.org).

The many beings are numberless; vowing to carry them across.
Greed, anger, and ignorance arise endlessly; vowing to cut off the mind road.
Dharma gates are countless; vowing to wake to them all.
Buddha's Way is all embracing; vowing to follow through.

3. Richard Davidson, quoted in Sharon Begley, *Train Your Mind, Change Your Brain: How a New Science Reveals Our Extraordinary Potential to Transform Ourselves* (New York: Ballantine Books, 2007), 239.

Dr. Davidson says, "Our findings clearly indicate that meditation can change the function of the brain in an enduring way."

4. Steve Hagen, *Buddhism Plain and Simple* (Boston: Tuttle Publishing, 1997), 7.

5. David Brazier, *The Feeling Buddha: A Buddhist Psychology of Character, Adversity and Passion* (New York: Palgrave and Macmillan, 2002), 42.

6. Hagen, *Buddhism Plain and Simple*, 8.

7. Eihei Dōgen Zenji, "Eihei Koso Hotsuganmon, Lofty Ancestor Eihei Dōgen's Verse for Arousing the Vow," in the Sutra Chant book, San Francisco Zen Center, CA, www.sfzc.org/sp_download/liturgy/29_Eihei_Koso_Hotsuganmon.pdf.

8. Hagen, *Buddhism Plain and Simple*, 9.

9. Eihei Dōgen Zenji, *Shōbōgenzō*, "On a Picture of a Rice Cake," in a presentation to the assembly in Japan, 1242, trans. Shasta Abbey, 2007, www.shastaabbey.org/1dogen/chapter/039gabyo.pdf.

10. The phrase "feeling the body in the body" is believed to be Buddha's words in the *Satipatthana Sutra, Discourse on the Four Establishments of Mindfulness*.

11. The description of qualities developed in meditation is adapted from Pema Chödrön, *Comfortable with Uncertainty: 108 Teachings on Cultivating Fearlessness and Compassion* (Boston: Shambhala Publications, 2003).

12. Pema Chödrön, *The Places That Scare You: A Guide to Fearlessness in Difficult Times* (Boston: Shambhala Publications, 2002), 29.

13. Ibid., 30.

14. This practice is used in the Fundamentals of Meditation class at Mind Roads Meditation Center, Saint Paul, MN (www.mindroads.com).

3. Taking Refuge

1. This description of "taking refuge" is from "A View on Buddhism," www.viewonbuddhism.org.

2. *Alcoholics Anonymous* (New York: Alcoholics Anonymous World Services, 1976), 59.

3. Reb Anderson, *Being Upright: Zen Meditation and the Bodhisattva Precepts* (Berkeley, CA: Rodmell Press, 2001), 41.

4. Thích Nhất Hanh, *The Heart of the Buddha's Teaching* (New York: Broadway Books, 1999), 167.

5. *Alcoholics Anonymous*, 55.

6. *Twelve Steps and Twelve Traditions*, 14th printing (New York: Alcoholics Anonymous World Services, 1976), 119–20.

7. Yongey Mingyur Rinpoche, *The Joy of Living: Unlocking the Secret and Science of Happiness* (New York: Three Rivers Press, 2007), 47.

8. Ibid., 48.

9. Anderson, *Being Upright,* 41.

10. Ibid., 43.

11. Hanh, *Heart of Buddha's Teaching,* 162.

12. Mingyur, *The Joy of Living,* 53.

13. Hanh, *Heart of Buddha's Teaching,* 163.

14. Anderson, *Being Upright,* 44.

15. Hanh, *Heart of Buddha's Teaching,* 162.

16. Anderson, *Being Upright,* 19.

17. Hanh, *Heart of Buddha's Teaching,* 167.

18. An *arahat* is a "Perfected One" who has overcome the three poisons of desire, hatred, and ignorance.

19. This story is adapted from the tale "The Story of the Abusive Brahmin Brothers," found in the Buddhist scripture *Dhammapada* (Sanskrit for "Words of Truth"); this text is regarded as the words of Buddha himself. A translation of verse 399, XXVI, can be found on the Web site of the Sangha of Buddhas (Jiddu Krishnamurti, Ramana Maharshi, Sri Ramakrishna, Swami Rama, Gautam Buddha, Lao Tzu, Mulla Nasruddin, Saint Kabir, Astavakra, Adi Shankaracharya), http://buddhasangha.blogspot.com/search/label/Gautam%20Buddha%20Dhammapada%20Stories.

20. Anderson, *Being Upright,* 46.

21. The teachings of Gautama Buddha were not recorded in written form until five hundred years after his death. Until that time, the stories of his teachings were passed on through oral tradition.

22. The Serenity Prayer is as follows:

> God, grant me the serenity to accept the things I cannot change,
> The courage to change the things I can,
> And the wisdom to know the difference.

23. Adapted from Hanh, *Heart of Buddha's Teachings,* 163.

4. Entering the Green Dragon's Cave

1. Merle A. Fossum and Marilyn J. Mason, *Facing Shame: Families in Recovery* (New York: W. W. Norton & Co., 1989).

2. Monica McGoldrick, John Pearce, and Joseph Giordano, eds., *Ethnicity and Family Therapy* (New York: Guilford Press, 1982), 313.

3. Ronda Dearing and others, study by University at Buffalo's Research Institute on Addictions (RIA) and George Mason University (Fairfax, VA, August 2005).

4. A. J. Mahari, *Borderline Personality Disorder,* www.borderlinepersonality.ca/.

5. Okakura-Kakuzo, *The Awakening of Japan* (New York: Century Co., 1904), 78.

6. *Twelve Steps and Twelve Traditions,* 14th printing (New York: Alcoholics Anonymous World Services, 1976), 44.

7. San Francisco Zen Center, "Teachings from Meditation in Recovery: Dhyana Paramita, the Perfection of Meditation," http://news.sfzc.org/content/view/578/461.

8. Stephen Batchelor, *Buddhism without Beliefs: A Contemporary Guide to Awakening* (New York: Riverhead, 1997), 67.

9. Dainin Katagiri, *Each Moment Is the Universe: Zen and the Way of Being Time,* ed. Andrea Martin (Boston: Shambhala Publications, 2007), 200.

10. *Samyutta Nikaya,* vol. 1, 71, quoted in Thích Nhất Hanh, *Teachings on Love* (Berkeley, CA: Parallax Press, 1997), 25.

11. Carl G. Jung, quoted in Lama Surya Das, *Awakening to the Sacred: Creating a Spiritual Life* (New York: Broadway Books/Random House, 1999), 62.

12. The Buddhist term *bodhisattva* means either "enlightened *(bodhi)* existence *(sattva)*" or "enlightenment-being" or "wisdom-being." It is the name given to anyone who, motivated by great compassion, wishes to attain enlightenment for the benefit of all living beings.

13. Reb Anderson, *Being Upright: Zen Meditation and the Bodhisattva Precepts* (Berkeley, CA: Rodmell Press, 2001), 184.

14. Bhante Henepola Gunaratana, *Mindfulness in Plain English* (Boston: Wisdom Publications, 2002), 3.

15. San Francisco Zen Center, "Teachings from Meditation in Recovery."

16. The Fourth Noble Truth of Buddhism is the last of the Four Pure Insights into the Way Things Are, taught by Buddha in the *Discourse on Turning the Wheel of the Dharma (Dhamma Cakka Pavattana Sutra).*

17. Steve Hagen, *Buddhism Plain and Simple* (Boston: Tuttle Publishing, 1997), 108.

18. Nonviolent Communication (NVC) is a specific approach to communicating—speaking and listening—that leads to giving from the heart and connecting with ourselves and with each other, developed by Marshall B. Rosenberg, *Nonviolent Communication: A Language of Life* (Encinitas, CA: PuddleDancer Press, 2003).

19. The questions presented here were developed by several members of a yearlong training, Entering the Way of Living Mindfully, at Mind Roads Meditation Center in 2009. The small group members are Maureen Ervin, Anne Murphy, and Ashley Zimmerman.

5. Placing Ourselves in the Cradle of Kindness

1. *Twelve Steps and Twelve Traditions,* 14th printing (New York: Alcoholics Anonymous World Services, 1976), 57.

2. Ibid, 58.

3. Pema Chödrön, *Comfortable with Uncertainty: 108 Teachings on Cultivating Fearlessness and Compassion* (Boston: Shambhala Publications, 2003), 185.

4. *Brahmaviharas* is the Pali and Sanskrit term for the Four Limitless Qualities.

5. Peter Harvey, *An Introduction to Buddhist Ethics* (Cambridge: Cambridge University Press, 2000), referenced in Wikipedia: The Free Encyclopedia, "Brahma-Vihara," http://en.wikipedia.org/wiki/Brahmavihara.

6. "Meeting upon the Path: An Interview with DaeJa Napier," *Northwest Dharma News* 11, no.6 (December/January 1999), http://brahmaviharas.org.

7. *Twelve and Twelve*, 59.

8. Yongey Mingyur Rinpoche, in a lecture at the University of Minnesota in Minneapolis, April 2009, described using mental recitation in meditation as "giving the monkey mind—unsettled, restless mind—a job."

9. Thích Nhất Hanh, *The Blooming of a Lotus: Guided Meditation for Achieving the Miracle of Mindfulness,* trans. Annabel Laity (Boston: Beacon Press, 1993), 8.

10. Ibid., 9.

11. Geneva Smitherman, *Talkin and Testifyin: The Language of Black America* (Detroit: Wayne State University Press, 1977), quoted in Michèle Foster, "Using Call-and-Response to Facilitate Language Mastery and Literacy Acquisition among African American Students," July 2002, www.cal.org/resources/digest/0204foster.html.

6. Turning Over a New Leaf

1. *Twelve Steps and Twelve Traditions,* 14th printing (New York: Alcoholics Anonymous World Services, 1976), 67.

2. Dainin Katagiri, *Each Moment Is the Universe: Zen and the Way of Being Time* (Boston: Shambhala Publications, 2007), 206.

3. Daniel Goleman, *Emotional Intelligence* (New York: Dell, 1995).

4. Sakyong Mipham Rinpoche, "Creating a Sustainable Internal Environment," August 2009, http://www.mipham.com/teachings.php?id=27.

Sakyong Mipham Rinpoche is the eldest son of the renowned Tibetan teacher Chögyam Trungpa Rinpoche. He serves as temporal and spiritual director of Shambhala, a global network of meditation and retreat centers. Sakyong—literally "earth-protector"—is a lineage holder of the Shambhala, Kagyü, and Nyingma sects of Tibetan Buddhism.

5. Ibid.

6. Sakyong Mipham Rinpoche, "The Four Maras Seduce and Bind Us to Suffering," *Spiritual Now,* September 30, 2008, www.spiritualnow.com/articles/214/1/The-Four-Maras-Seduce-and-Bind-us-to-Suffering/Page1.html.

7. Ibid.

8. *Alcoholics Anonymous* (New York: Alcoholics Anonymous World Services, 1976), 58.

9. Katagiri, *Each Moment*, 205.

10. Har Dayal, *Boddhisattva Doctrine in Buddhist Sanskrit Literature* (London: Motilal Banarsidass Press, 1999).

11. Katagiri, *Each Moment*, 201.

12. Questions are adapted from an assignment for the Dismantling Habituated Patterns class at Mind Roads Meditation Center, developed in collaboration with Byakuren Judith Ragir, www.judithragir.org.

7. Vowing with the Help of All Beings

1. Dainin Katagiri, *Each Moment Is the Universe: Zen and the Way of Being Time* (Boston: Shambhala Publications, 2007), 202.

2. *Twelve Steps and Twelve Traditions,* 14th printing (New York: Alcoholics Anonymous World Services, 1976), 70.

3. Pema Chödrön, "Bodhichitta and Aspiration," Web lecture, City Retreat, Berkeley, CA, Shambhala Center, www.shambhala.org.

4. Ibid.

5. Buddhist monks, nuns, and lay practitioners take the Bodhisattva Vows, reciting the following:

> Beings are numberless, vowing to save them,
> Suffering is inexhaustible, vowing to end it,
> Dharma gates are boundless, vowing to open them,
> The Buddha Way is unsurpassable, vowing to become it.

6. Definition of the word *vow* is from www.britannica.com.

7. Chödrön, "Bodhichitta and Aspiration."

8. Definition of *gāthā* is based on the Sanskrit word *udāna*, meaning "an inspired utterance," www.britannica.com.

8. Finding Pearls in the Dust-Bin

1. *Twelve Steps and Twelve Traditions,* 14th printing (New York: Alcoholics Anonymous World Services, 1976), 84.

2. Eihei Dōgen Zenji, "Eihei Koso Hotsuganmon, Lofty Ancestor Eihei Dōgen's Verse for Arousing the Vow" in the Sutra Chant book, San Francisco Zen Center, CA, http://sfzc.org/sp_download/liturgy/29_Eihei_Koso_Hotsuganmon.pdf.

3. Shantideva (sometimes Śāntideva) was an eighth-century Indian Buddhist. He is particularly renowned as the author of the *Bodhicharyavatara,* translated as *A Guide to the Bodhisattva's Way of Life.* It is a long poem describing the process of enlightenment

from the first thought to full buddhahood and is still studied by many Buddhists today. A commentary by Pema Chödrön was published as *No Time to Lose: A Timely Guide to the Way of the Bodhisattva* (Boston: Shambhala Publications, 2005).

This translation is from Shantideva, "Miracle of Awakening," in *Bodhicharyavatara (A Guide to the Bodhisattva's Way of Life),* quoted in Jack Kornfield, ed., adapted by Eknath Easwaran, *Teachings of the Buddha* (Boston: Shambhala Publications, 2007), 132.

4. *Twelve and Twelve,* 81.

5. Reb Anderson, presentation at retreat, Minnesota Zen Meditation Center, Minneapolis, MN, April 2008.

6. Reb Anderson, *Being Upright: Zen Meditation and the Bodhisattva Precepts* (Berkeley, CA: Rodmell Press, 2001), 30.

7. *Twelve and Twelve,* 89.

8. In the *Sudatta Sutta,* Buddha discusses the four kinds of bliss, including the bliss of ownership, the bliss of wealth, the bliss of being debtless, and the bliss of blamelessness.

9. Anderson, *Being Upright,* 30.

10. *Twelve and Twelve,* 84.

11. Anderson, *Being Upright,* 30.

12. "Prayer of Atonement," from Bodhisattva Initiation Ceremony in Buddhism, quoted in Anderson, *Being Upright,* 28.

9. Standing on the Ground of Our Deeds

1. Bhikkhu Ñānamoli and Bhikkhu Bodhi, trans., "Ambalatthikarahulovada Sutta: Advice to Rāhula at Ambalatthikā," in *The Middle Length Discourses of the Buddha: A New Translation of the Majjhima Nikāya* (Boston: Wisdom Publications, 1995), 524.

2. Ibid.

3. Ibid., 526.

4. Ibid., 525.

5. *Twelve Steps and Twelve Traditions,* 14th printing (New York: Alcoholics Anonymous World Services, 1976), 91.

6. This rendition is Thích Nhất Hanh's version of a practice advised in "Maha Rahulovada Sutta: Big Advice to Rahula," trans. Ven. Anzan Hoshin-roshi and Tory Cox, www.wwzc.org/translations/mahaRahulovada.htm.

7. Richard Davidson, study at Promega Corporation (WI), 1997, cited in Stephen Hall, "Is Buddhism Good for Your Health?" *New York Times,* September 14, 2003.

The results suggest that meditation may indeed leave a discernible and lasting imprint on the minds and bodies of its practitioners. In the Promega employees who practiced meditation for two months, the Wisconsin researchers detected significant increases in activity in several areas of the left prefrontal cortex—heightened activity that persisted for at least four months after the experiment, when the subjects were tested again.

8. Thanissaro Bhikkhu, trans., "Ambalatthikarahulovada Sutta: Instructions to Rāhula," in *Majjhima Nikāya 61*, www.vipassana.com/canon/majjhima/mn61.php.

9. *Twelve and Twelve*, 91.

10. Gregg Krech, *Naikan: Gratitude, Grace, and the Japanese Art of Self-Reflection* (Berkeley, CA: Stone Bridge Press, 2002), 26.

11. Noble silence is often practiced in Zen Buddhist retreats (called *sesshin*, a period of intensive meditation) where speaking or interacting with others is restricted.

12. "Upajjhatthana Sutta" [Subjects for contemplation] in *Handful of Leaves: An Anthology from the Anguttara Nikāya*, vol. 3, trans. Thanissaro Bhikkhu (Redwood City, CA: Sati Center for Buddhist Studies, 2003).

The *five remembrances* are five facts upon which all people are advised to reflect often, whether lay or monastic, male or female. These five subjects for contemplation (as translated by Thanissaro Bhikkhu) are

1. I am subject to aging, have not gone beyond aging.
2. I am subject to illness, have not gone beyond illness.
3. I am subject to death, have not gone beyond death.
4. I will grow different, separate from all that is dear and appealing to me.
5. I am the owner of my actions, heir to my actions, born of my actions, related through my actions, and have my actions as arbitrator.

13. *Twelve and Twelve*, 90.

10. Making Conscious Contact

1. *Twelve Steps and Twelve Traditions,* 14th printing (New York: Alcoholics Anonymous World Services, 1976), 99.

2. Ibid., 105.

3. The term "buddha-mind" refers to the seeds of an enlightened mind, or essence of goodness within all sentient beings.

4. *Twelve and Twelve*, 98.

5. Shunryu Suzuki, *Not Always So: Practicing the True Spirit of Zen,* ed. Edward Espe Brown (New York: Quill/Harper-Collins Publishers, 2003), 5.

6. Ibid.

7. *Twelve and Twelve*, 99.

8. Adapted from Mark Epstein, *Thoughts without a Thinker: Psychotherapy from a Buddhist Perspective,* paperback ed. (New York: Basic Books, 1996), 43.

9. Arthur Braverman, *Mud & Water: The Collected Teachings of Zen Master Bassui* (Boston: Wisdom Publications, 2002), 28.

10. *Twelve and Twelve,* 100.

11. Thích Nhất Hanh, *The Heart of the Buddha's Teaching* (New York: Broadway Books, 1999), 187.

Hanh is referring to a Buddhist scripture called *The Lotus Sutra (Saddharma Pundarīka).*

12. Thích Nhất Hanh, "Writing from Plum Village," 2007, www.plumvillage.org/letters-from-thay.

13. All four descriptions of meditation techniques have been adapted from Yongey Mingyur Rinpoche, *The Joy of Living: Unlocking the Secret and Science of Happiness* (New York: Three Rivers Press, 2007).

14. Rinpoche, *The Joy of Living,* 55.

15. Ibid.

16. Ibid., 144.

17. Hanh, "Writing from Plum Village."

Plum Village (Làng Mai) is a Buddhist meditation center in the Dordogne in southern France. It was founded by Vietnamese monk Thích Nhất Hanh and his colleague Bhikkhuni Chân Không in 1982. Plum Village houses approximately sixty-five monks and laypersons, as well as being Thích Nhất Hanh's residence.

11. Remembering Our True Face

1. Thomas Byrom, trans., "Crossing the Stream," in *The Dhammapada: The Sayings of the Buddha* (New York: Alfred A. Knopf, 1976), quoted in Jack Kornfield, ed., *Teachings of the Buddha* (Boston: Shambhala Publications, 2007), 34.

2. Thích Nhất Hanh, *The Heart of the Buddha's Teaching* (New York: Broadway Books, 1999), 27.

3. Byrom, trans., *Dhammapada,* quoted in Kornfield, ed., *Teachings of the Buddha,* 34.

4. Hahn, *Heart of Buddha's Teaching,* 62.

5. Pema Chödrön, *The Places That Scare You: A Guide to Fearlessness in Difficult Times* (Boston: Shambhala Publications, 2002), 4.

Chödrön defines the "soft spot of the heart" as the innate ability to love and care about things.

6. Yongey Mingyur Rinpoche, *The Joy of Living: Unlocking the Secret and Science of Happiness* (New York: Three Rivers Press, 2007), 189.

7. Ibid., 191.

8. Ibid., 190.

9. *Twelve Steps and Twelve Traditions,* 14th printing (New York: Alcoholics Anonymous World Services, 1976), 115.

10. John Blofeld, trans., *The Zen Teachings of Huang Po,* quoted in Kornfield, ed., *Teachings of the Buddha,* 199.

11. Thích Nhất Hanh, *Teachings on Love* (Berkeley, CA: Parralla Press, 1998), 69.

ABOUT THE AUTHOR

✠

Thérèse Jacobs-Stewart, M.A., L.P., has been a practicing psychotherapist, meditation teacher, and international consultant for more than twenty-five years. In 2004, she founded Mind Roads Meditation Center, a neighborhood practice center integrating contemplative practices from both East and West and home of the Saint Paul, Minnesota, chapter of Twelve Steps and Mindfulness meetings.

Jacobs-Stewart has studied with Tibetan Buddhist monks in Nepal and India, Carmelite contemplatives in a monastery in Arizona, and the Soto Zen community at Green Gulch Farm Zen Center, San Francisco, California.

For more information about Thérèse Jacobs-Stewart and her teaching schedule, see www.mindroads.com.